MOON SPELLS

DIANE AHLQUIST

Illustrations by Patty Volz

Adams Media
New York London Toronto Sydney New Delhi

Dedication

I dedicate this book to all those who hold it in their hands—to those who believe there is more than what we experience on the physical plane and to all who are adventuresome and are influenced by the Moon and her positive energy. You are the seekers, you are the pathfinders. No matter what your age, you are the voices of the new age . . . you are the true magick in life.

adamsmedia

Adams Media
An Imprint of Simon & Schuster, Inc.
100 Technology Center Drive
Stoughton, MA 02072

For information about special discounts for bulk purchases, please contact Simon & Schuster Special Sales at 1-866-506-1949 or business@simonandschuster.com.

The Simon & Schuster Speakers Bureau can bring authors to your live event. For more information or to book an event contact the Simon & Schuster Speakers Bureau at 1-866-248-3049 or visit our website at www.simonspeakers.com.

Interior illustrations by Patty Volz

Manufactured in China

10 9 8 7 6 5 4 3 2 1

Library of Congress Cataloging-in-Publication Data has been applied for.

ISBN 978-1-58062-695-8

Contents

Acknowledgments

There are some people who you cannot thank enough and one of those is Claire Gerus, my editor. To her I express appreciation and love. Also, Laura MacLaughlin, Kate McBride, and all at Adams Media for their efforts to make this book responsive to the needs of the reader.

Naturally, my mother, Rosemarie, who always thought I was wonderful but different!

To my sister, Marie, for her research and insights of the metaphysical. To my nephews, Daniel and Johnny Frenden, for their blessed thoughts.

To Adrian Volney, for his patience and considerate nature as I pursue my interests and for understanding why I must have a moon circle in our backyard! To the Volney children, for their smiling faces and happy dispositions.

A special thanks to Patty Volz, a dear friend, who unselfishly contributed her artwork to these pages. A job well done and a God-given gift I am glad you are pursuing.

Denise Satter . . . the cover art looks wonderful! You made the book come alive.

Laura Nelson . . . over twenty years ago, I thought you were one of the finest people I had ever met. To this day, that truth remains the same.

Also, to . . .

Dave Stern . . . always my lighthouse in the storm of life.

Debi Albert, a friend who supported me unconditionally and always wished me success.

Roger Goff . . . as always, your words of wisdom and knowledge made the difference.

Kathy Greager . . . a true Moon advocate and my favorite Pisces.

Inger Svenson . . . your Swedish energy and insights enlightened me.

Pat Samuels . . . for your invaluable comments and interest in things that are new to you.

Rahelio . . . for reminding me to keep everything in the circle.

Joe Lubow . . . an angel in disguise.

Mike Seery . . . just talking to you encourages me and gives me confidence in what I do.

Carolyn Drogan . . . "I think of you more than you know. Namaste"

Brandi Keown . . . you make the state of Virginia shine.

Frank Smith . . . whose houseboat was my lodging while I wrote much of this book.

Blessings to: Robert Irwin, Brenda Brock, and Charlotte, Desmond, and Andrew Campbell.

All of my clients and friends whose names I would thank individually if it were not for the limitations of space.

And finally, to the essence of all the ascended masters for daily guidance they give me in meditation.

Introduction

I was named after the Moon Goddess, Diana. Even so, while I was growing up, I paid no more attention to our closest celestial neighbor than any other child. Then, about ten years ago, a friend of mine who worked at the police department pointed out that her emergency calls were heavier on and around the full Moon. This prompted me to wonder about the Moon's influence on my life.

I had kept a journal for many years, and on one ambitious day I went back over my old entries. To my surprise, I discovered a profound connection between the Moon's phases and the important events in my past. The projects or romances that "worked" were started under a new Moon; most negative events in my life took place under a full Moon. Diets never worked when the Moon was waxing—but business thrived.

My divorce (which proceeded with no conflict or ill feelings) was initiated under a waning Moon. My intuition was more accurate at a full Moon, my energy lowest when the Moon was dark. Thoroughly fascinated, I began researching and experimenting with techniques to take advantage of this new discovery. Once I found techniques that worked for me, the obvious next step was to see if they would work for others.

I have now been doing "intuitive counseling" for over twenty years. Throughout that time I recognized I was frequently using the phases of the Moon to help my clients get their lives under control. I provided rituals for them to perform as a means of helping them to better themselves for the good of all and without interfering with anyone else. Although I technically never put a word to these rites, they were what some would consider spells . . . Moon Spells.

Skeptical?

Let me tell you about one of those clients—and her brother, who met my client and me for dinner one evening. This gentleman talked about nothing but himself all night. He was clearly unhappy and exceptionally frustrated at his lack of employment.

I asked him in which phase of the Moon he planned his interviews.

He rolled his eyes. "Looking at the Moon isn't going to get me a job," he growled.

I smiled. "I see you have your date book with you," I said. "Just for fun, why don't we review the dates of your interviews for the last three months." He reluctantly agreed.

It was no surprise to me when the calendar showed that all his previous appointments had taken place under a waning Moon—a time for releasing and letting go . . . not starting new endeavors. When I explained this to him, he remained skeptical and uninterested.

Later on, he mentioned that he had another interview that very week. I knew that, again, the Moon was waning. I asked him if he could postpone the interview a while longer until the Moon would be waxing (an ideal time for job hunting).

At his sister's urging, he acquiesced. Then, the day before his rescheduled interview (again largely due to his sister's prompting), the three of us performed a group spell for employment—the same one you'll find later on in this book.

At the interview the next day, he was told he didn't qualify for the job. He rushed right home and called me, sounding almost happy. "You're full of beans," he told me (or words to that effect). "The Moon and these spells have no special powers."

The following morning, the gentleman with whom he had interviewed the day before contacted him. Another position had become available with a better salary. He took the job . . . but refused to acknowledge it might have had anything to do with the spell we performed.

Nevertheless, he suddenly decided to mention he had been without a girlfriend for over two years. Was he, in fact, hinting about a spell that could assist in finding him a mate? No, not Mr. Skeptic!

Smiling, I told him about the love spells. Again, he agreed to try them—but only "to prove once and for all that this is nonsense."

He waited for a new Moon (the proper phase to undertake a new romance) and recited the spell when he was alone.

The next evening, I found another sarcastic message on my answering machine from him, saying that he'd failed to meet the love of his life and that all these spells had been a waste of time and effort. I called him back and explained that the spells usually took longer than a single day. And after waiting two years for the results of his own efforts, I didn't think a couple of days was so much to ask. It actually took two weeks.

Mr. Skeptic met a lady at a yard sale, whom he eventually married. Last I heard, they were doing well—and wanted to know if I had any suggestions for a spell for a new house and family!

The book you hold in your hands outlines the same kind of simple spells and techniques that helped Mr. Skeptic achieve his life goals. Used in conjunction with the energy provided by the Moon's five basic phases (New, Waxing, Full, Waning, and Dark), these "Moon Spells" can help you overcome the challenges you face in your own life.

Ancient civilizations were very respectful of the Moon's power: They planted crops according to the Moon's phases, paid homage to her in countless rituals, and celebrated her with their most festive holidays.

Even today, when we know her power on a more practical level (the cause of ocean tides, her influence on women's menstrual cycles), we all remain fascinated and intrigued by the mystery and beauty of the full Moon in the night sky.

Today, it's virtually impossible to pick up any publication pertaining to the use of the Moon's phases without becoming an amateur astrologer. I have great respect for the Zodiac and the wealth of information one can derive from it, but not everyone has the time to study or practice it.

Rather than relying heavily on astrology, *Moon Spells* simply focuses on an understanding of the five basic phases of the Moon and how to apply them to your life. The spells will allow you to relax and look at life's challenges with greater clarity, to reach an altered state of consciousness. By tapping into that level of consciousness, you'll find a wealth of information to guide you and give you the ability to perform what some would call *magick*.

Still skeptical?

For a chance at peace and happiness, I think it's well worth trying the techniques in this book. You may transform your life. At worst, you'll spend a few nights looking at our beautiful Moon.

How to Use This Book

Read the section entitled "Preparation" before beginning any spell. Familiarize yourself with the general concepts in the sections on when, where, and how to perform spells. Flip through the enhancements section as well—the extras described therein that will help you to relax and reach an altered state more easily.

Diagrams will show you different placements for either individuals or groups. If you're doing group spells, this section is extremely important: Read it thoroughly and take the time to understand the way these sessions are to be conducted. When guiding other individuals, you must make sure you have a firm grasp of what you are doing or the process will have a weak and chaotic energy, and you will lose the confidence of the others in your group.

Then turn to the Table of Contents and find the spells that most intrigue you. Each spell suggests the proper enhancements, formation to cast, and the optimum phase of the Moon under which it should be performed.

If you discover something in one of the spells that does not sit right with you—even if it is only a single word or phrase—change it to make yourself more comfortable.

The Lunar Calendar provides a daily picture of which phase the Moon is in, starting at a full Moon. To keep the Calendar from ever becoming outdated, we have used a general format of how the phases will make their passage. Start at the full Moon and follow it all the way through.

Don't pressure yourself to memorize details, such as what color candles to use or what gemstones best suit your situation. That's what this book is for. Refer back to it as often as you like. Memorization of your favorite spells isn't necessary either. If you don't want to carry the whole book around, make a copy of the spell you use most often and carry that. Above all, take your time and don't rush the process.

This book promotes no specific belief system and requires no extensive knowledge of magick. It is a nondenominational, spiritual approach. The only thing it requires is that you believe in God, a Higher Power, or the balance of Nature. The spells or rituals are a blend of different belief systems and different rites. There are those who do not believe in the mixing of such beliefs. However, I have found that a combination of the vibrations from different philosophies brings powerful results. In fact, the very book you hold in your hands this moment is the result of a Moon Spell I have performed!

Other books on the market today that deal with Moon rituals and Moon power fall into two categories: those dependent on astrology and those written by people practicing Wicca, the religion of nature.

To fully understand how astrological signs apply to the Moon's phases requires an extensive explanation of astrology itself and a belief in its guiding principles. The books that treat the Moon from this perspective are typically split in half: first focusing on astrology and then on the Moon.

Those books that present the Moon as a focus of pagan or Wiccan beliefs are also split personalities, again having to explain their two main subjects separately. By no means is there anything wrong with such beliefs—their spiritual roots, their focus on nature, and their intention are true. Although you will find similarities to some Wiccan beliefs, this book is not Wiccan and is not a book of witchcraft. The fact that I refer to these rituals as spells should not alarm or offend. It is merely a catchy word to explain the appeal to the universe or the God of your understanding for some extra help. The word "spell" can be easily replaced by: Moon ceremonies, Moon observances, or sacred Moon rites.

Many religions have their version of rites using tools such as candles, incense, statues, and holy water. The use of color and representation is also significant to certain religious groups. So performing what I refer to as a spell is not much different than someone praying at a home altar to their favorite saint with candles lit and holy water nearby.

I have never judged anyone else's beliefs. I feel that all those who believe in a higher power than ourselves, have respect for each other and the planet, and believe in not intentionally causing harm to someone else all answer to the same Divine. It is my hope and prayer that someday all religions will respect other belief systems and recognize the vanity of believing that one specific religion is the only true religion on the planet. Let us all unite and love one another. Is this not the basis of every religion on the earth? At least there is this commonality.

Performing these spells, in my opinion, is not in opposition to anyone's religion or beliefs. They are experiments with vibration, energy, the elements, and an appeal to the subconscious mind. These acts are a strong call of assistance to whatever or whoever you believe our maker to be.

Anyone can pick up this book and immediately start utilizing it to access the Moon as a source of strength and transformation for a more positive lifestyle. The emphasis in *Moon Spells* on the five basic phases of the Moon, which most of us are somewhat familiar with, sets it apart from other books on the subject. Those phases are: full, waning, dark, new, and waxing. Detailed information about these phases can be found in the section, "When to Perform Your Spell."

PART I
Preparing for Your Spell

Introduction

Spells require thought, preparation, and an understanding of the proper approach, which will allow you to spark the magick in which you will be invoking. An organized ritual is a successful ritual. Working with the elements of nature, timing, and certain configurations puts us in sync with the universal life force energy. The wise spell caster waits until everything is in order and does not rush the natural flow of energy that moves like a current in the unseen. Harmonize yourself with these preparatory details and you will experience the curious and mystic properties they conjure. Act proficiently in your efforts and you will be rewarded with the results of a task well done.

• 1 •

When to Perform Your Spell

When conducting these spells, use the phases of the Moon to set the pace. Be patient and wait for the proper phase or you may not get the results you seek. I include the best phase or phases of the Moon in which to perform your spells along with the spell itself for easy reference. However, here is additional data that will give you a better understanding of how I determined the best phase of the Moon for each particular spell. This will also be of benefit to you when creating your own spells for any occasion.

The Phases of the Moon

New

Sometimes called the crescent Moon, when you can see the very first sliver of light in the sky. This phase promotes new beginnings, new endeavors, and new relationships. It is a time for making positive changes, looking for fresh career opportunities, and planting seeds of ideas that will be harvested later.

Waxing

In this phase, the Moon appears to be growing in size, shifting from new to full as though it's gaining strength. It makes sense, then, that this is a good time to focus on increasing things of your own—your knowledge, bank accounts, relationships. It's a time to think about pregnancy, to increase communications of all types, whether for business or pleasure. Deal with legal matters if you want financial gain. This phase promotes healing.

Full

The Moon's most powerful phase, when we see her entire illuminated face. This is a time of fulfillment, activity, increased psychic ability, for perfecting ideas, "getting your act together," celebrations, or renewing commitments to people or projects. The best time for spells of any kind.

Waning

The Moon is decreasing in size as it journeys from full to dark. The waning Moon is a time of decrease, release, letting go, and completion. An excellent time to begin dieting, breaking bad habits, breaking off relationships, or dealing with legal matters.

Dark

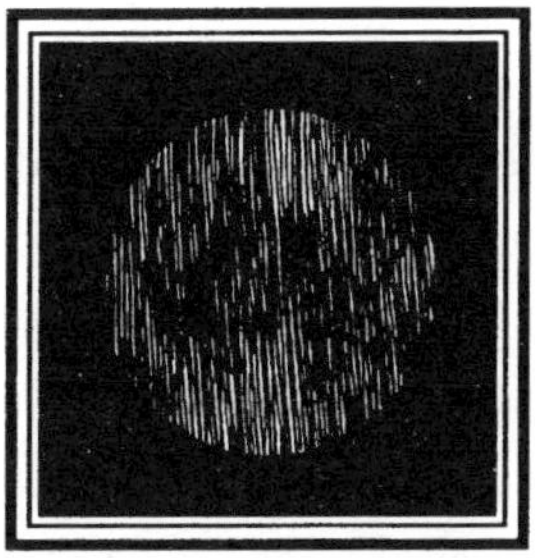

The two or three days when the Moon is not visible in the sky at all. The dark Moon and the new Moon are often considered the same phase, but for our purposes I have separated the two. On an average calendar, the dark Moon is usually indicated by a black spot on your calendar. However, the dark Moon occurs on the day it is marked as well as one day before and one day after. This is a good time for discarding things in your life you do not want, contemplating what you have already accomplished, and what you want to accomplish in the future. An excellent cycle to find time for yourself, or if you're so inclined, an ideal time for seclusion.

Moons of the Year

Every month has one full Moon. When there are two full Moons in one month, this is called a blue Moon. Every calendar year has one blue Moon. Ancient people assigned different names for the Moons of each month.

Different cultures gave the Moon different titles to express what the Moon meant to them in a given month. Some of the Moon names make common sense, while others may make no sense at all unless you know the logic behind it.

January

Common Name: Wolf Moon

Uncommon Name: Chaste Moon—Calls for cleansing and renewal as the new year begins; it is the time for starting over, washing away the past, and fresh beginnings.

February

Common Name: Ice Moon

Uncommon Name: Hunger Moon—Winter's supplies depleted, the yearning for spring is a hunger of the soul as well as the belly.

March

Common Name: Storm Moon

Uncommon Name: Worm Moon—The thawing of the earth brings a renewal of life as the earthworms break the soil and emerge from the damp earth in the moonlight.

April

Common Name: Growing Moon

Uncommon Name: Pink Moon—The spring fills the meadows with the pink heads of wildflowers and new grasses.

May

Common Name: Hare Moon

Uncommon Name: Milk Moon—The birth of animals, domestic and wild, brings forth the mother's milk, the life-giver, and first food of man and beast.

June

Common Name: Mead Moon

Uncommon Name: Dyad Moon—The Moon of the month of Gemini, this period honors twins and the sacred marriage of the god and goddess, bringing two into one.

July

Common Name: Hay Moon

Uncommon Name: Wort Moon—*Wort* being an ancient word for herbs, it is the Moon for gathering of herbs, replenishing the stores of medicinal plants, and drying them in the heat of summer for the long winter to come.

August

Common Name: Corn Moon

Uncommon Name: Dispute Moon—The earth mother gives birth to bountiful harvest; with full bellies and hope for continuation, we settle our disputes and put away old anger as we look forward to the long, peaceful winter to come.

September

Common Name: Harvest Moon

Uncommon Name: Vine Moon—The Celtic Moon of exhilaration, driven by forces of work to obtain completion—of the harvest, the winemaking, and insight for the future.

October

Common Name: Blood Moon (a time of hunting)

Uncommon Name: Shedding Moon—the Moon where the deer shed their antlers and begin the rut—the compelling drive to create new life that supersedes the death of winter.

November

Common Name: Snow Moon

Uncommon Name: Tree Moon—The Celtic tree months of the Reed and the Elder tree overlap with the reed representing the Moon of silence, inner workings, and strength and the elder representing the Moon of completion; the days shorten as the end of the year draws near.

December

Common Name: Cold Moon

Uncommon Name: Oak Moon—Sacred tree of the ancients, strong enough to withstand the harshest winter, renewal of the new year, straddling the old, dark year and the new light year two worlds, as the oak tree's roots are in the dark earth and its branches are in the sky.

Days of the Week to Conduct Rituals

The day of the week on which you execute a spell can also have an impact on your ceremony. The day of the week is not as important as the phases of the Moon; however, if you are able to coordinate the right day with the right phase of the Moon, that makes it all the more powerful. For example, a spell for attracting a lover is best done on a Friday when the Moon is full, new, or waxing. But if the Moon is not in the right phase for relationships on Friday, do not be overly concerned. Proceed with the spell and do not worry about what day of the week it is. The weekdays equate to adding a pinch of salt in a stew. It may make it a bit tastier but will not make a significant difference. Do not wait for months till everything is in perfect order. If everything else in essence is perfect and the day of the week you were hoping for is not workable, there is a higher purpose at work. The day you perform your spell will be perfect for you.

Days of the Week for Spells and Rituals

Day	Ruling Planet	Best For
Monday	Moon	Psychic endeavors or impressions, invoking power, creative ideas, divine/inspirational messages, healing
Tuesday	Mars	Sexual encounters, protection, building strength of mind and body, confidence
Wednesday	Mercury	Career/job issues, intellectual pursuits, travel planning, research
Thursday	Jupiter	Finances, legal matters, spirituality, development
Friday	Venus	Romantic attraction, all relationships, reconciliation, physical makeovers, beautifying your environment
Saturday	Saturn	Home-related issues, brainstorming future project, committing to personal goals, weight loss, releasing bad habits, endings of any kind—relationships, etc.
Sunday	Sun	Healing of body, mind, soul, management/decision-making, Insights to problem solving, divine intervention/miracles, special friendships

• 2 •

Lunar Calendar

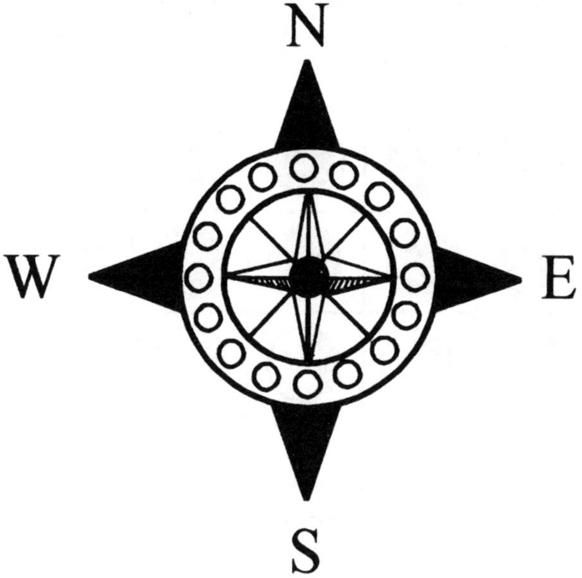

The lunation of the Moon is approximately twenty-nine-and-a-half days starting from a full Moon and continuing until the next full Moon. To give you an idea of how the lunation occurs, I have included an approximate idea of the Moon phase process. For simplification, day twenty-nine-and-a-half will be considered day thirty.

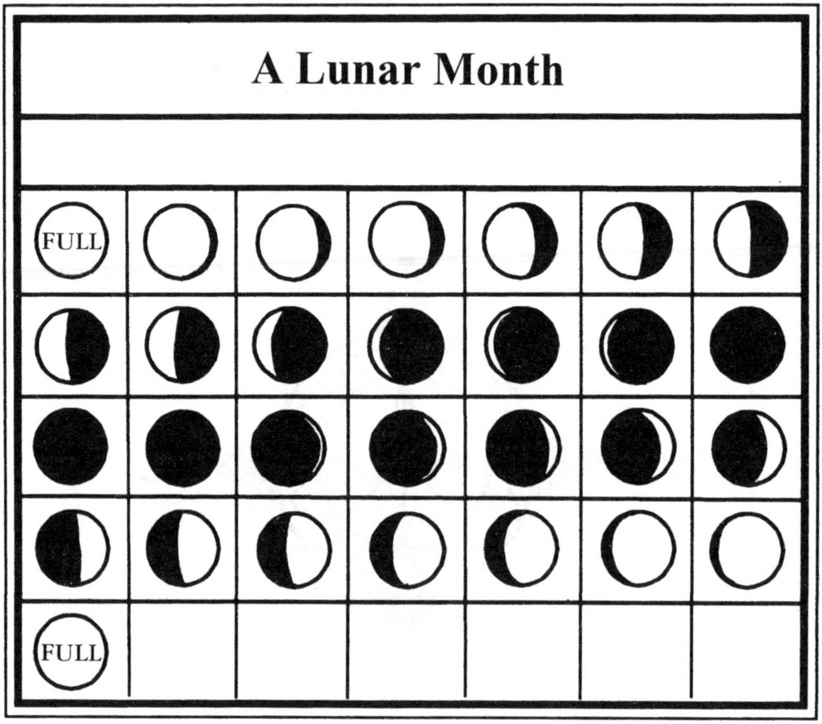
A Lunar Month
FULL
FULL

3

Where to Conduct Your Spells

Location is important, but you must be practical and do what is best for you. There are pros and cons to everything, and where to cast a spell is no different. There are those who will say there is nothing like the outside to spin you magick. However, if you live in the middle of downtown Los Angeles, Detroit, Atlanta, or New York, that is not a very wise choice. As we live in modern times of condominium life, the noise of speeding cars and construction vehicles outside may be too chaotic. In medieval times, for example, things like ambulances, airplanes, railroad trains, and automobile horns were not a concern. Therefore, think in the now and not about what our ancestors' situations were.

Consider your specific location and determine what alternatives you have available.

Inside

It is easier to conduct spells inside, due to the fact that wind will not keep blowing out your candles, you have electricity for music, there is privacy and also safety.

As you are accessing the powers of the Moon, try to find a spot where you can see the Moon, if possible. But above all, be comfortable. If there is a room in your home where you can see the Moon but you are not relaxed in that area, do not use it.

If you're conducting your spell during the day or are someplace without windows or any view of the sky, use a representation of the Moon. A picture of the Moon works well (feel free to draw your own) or any item that represents the Moon.

You can purchase a terra cotta Moon decoration at most garden centers or make one out of cardboard or anything you have available. A Moon pendant or pin would do. Be creative; anything *you* feel that represents the Moon is perfect for *you*.

Keep in mind, your privacy is a must. There should be no one else in the room with you unless they are directly participating in this ritual. If you have a large family and have a difficult time finding a place to be alone, you can always opt for the bathroom. It may sound comical, but I performed one of my best spells in the bathroom at a Holiday Inn as I was sharing a room with a friend who was not like-minded.

Outside

To do a spell outside is excellent as you are surrounded by nature. However, the majority of people do not have acres of land where they can be assured privacy. Even in a park or on a beach, there is the probability of you attracting onlookers and people passing by.

A backyard is workable, but if you have noisy neighbors, barking dogs, or a delivery person that may show up unexpectedly, it is not a good idea. Remember that you should not be trying to gain attention. Be discreet, and the power is more effective.

If you are one of the lucky ones who has a privacy fence or lots of land around you, you may give it try. The use of candles may not work if it is a windy day. (See the candle section for more details on how to cope with this situation.)

Whatever you do, make sure you always feel safe. If you cast your spell in the evening and are afraid someone will sneak up on you, it will defeat the purpose. Why add stress to your spell?

Usually a group of people is better for outdoor spells. Weigh the positives and the negatives and make a choice. I have performed spells outside as well as inside, and the results have not been more successful one way or the other. I must admit, though, if you have the opportunity to perform magick amidst nature, do venture to do so. The experience is very enchanting.

Tree Magick

For those who are able to utilize the wonders of the outside world in an area that has many trees, you may want to conduct your spell under or near a special tree. It could be a tree you just get a "good feeling" from or a specific tree you seek that has a special quality. I conduct many spells under an orange tree in my own backyard.

Many cultures feel trees have curative properties and can dispel negative energy from a person without harming the tree. This is why sometimes just a walk through a national forest or the local park can calm you.

If you perform a spell near a special tree, take a moment and feel the energy from that particular tree. Thank the tree for the vibration that it is giving to you. Native Americans and other cultures believe that a tree embodies a living spirit.

Don't be surprised, but hugging trees is not as uncommon as one would think. Sometimes a tree has a specific quality that we need—something that has been depleted within our own bodies. Hence, we have a need to put back that vital force. These are the trees we are usually drawn to, as they can rejuvenate us without taking away from themselves.

Example: If your interest in romance has been virtually zero due to conditions in your life like overworking, traveling, or just being without a partner, you may have the need to put yourself near or even hug an oak tree. The oak is said to increase sexuality!

"Nothing ventured nothing gained."

Following is a small list of trees expressing qualities and essences that are said to be of their nature.

Ash: peace, protection, prosperity, strength

Birch: new beginnings, healing of wounds and burns

Cedar: courage, longevity, wealth, self-esteem, purification

Coconut Palm: purity, honor, relaxation

Cypress: past life issues, comfort, protection; eases the loss of anything

Elder: transformation and change, peaceful sleep, self-confidence

Elm: protection and meditation; stops slander

Eucalyptus: healing, protection, moon affinity

Lilac: activate chakras (energy centers), healing of back pain

Lime: divination, development, cleansing

Magnolia: fidelity, changes, relaxation and calmness

Maple: longevity, love, money

Myrtle: fertility, balance, youth, riches

Oak: increasing sexuality, luck, strength

Pear: clarity, energy, confidence, reduction of stress

Pecan: career issues and job seeking, money, discipline

Pine: prosperity, purification, health, exorcism

Plum: love and healing, self-confidence

Poplar: astral projection, wisdom, mental healing, starting over

Walnut: depression, healing, heals infertility

Willow: wishes coming true, seductiveness, protection, energy to the sick

The magick in trees does not have to be activated only when carrying out Moon spells, but can be accessed anytime as a natural wealth of refreshment to your body, mind, and spirit. Always thank the tree in silence with a nod of your head for allowing you to receive its special essential qualities and for absorbing your negativity. For the record, the tree is not harmed by this process—it shakes your energy away via the elements and is refreshed within seconds.

Which Direction to Face

Another gift of nature and an important factor to consider when initiating a Moon spell is the direction in which to face. Compass directions north, south, east, and west are very significant when casting a spell. By facing the proper direction, you are utilizing the vibration or energy that it offers. The powers of the four directions are a free gift of nature that is often overlooked.

You can also think of the four directions as the four winds. You can "bring up the winds" from the north, south, east, and west. This means you will still stand facing a compass point, but will invoke the energy to blow toward you in the form of a gust. By not bringing up the winds, the flow of the vital forces are far more gentle, which is often necessary. It depends on the type of spell whether you only face a specific direction or you face that direction and also bring up the winds. One might compare it to an electric fan with two speeds. The flow of air is coming from the same source, but you control how quickly or slowly it reaches you.

Also, bear in mind that you most likely will not actually *feel* the wind that you have summoned. However, the invisible activity through the air will make its way to your spell area and serve you far beyond your realm of thought. There is magick in the air!

For each individual spell in this book, I provide you with the direction in which to face. I also suggest whether to bring up the winds or not and provide you the invocations on how to do so. In addition, for spells you create on your own, as well as for your own general information, I have included the following details about the vibration that emanates from each compass direction.

NORTH corresponds to the element of earth. Face north for health issues, healing of the body, spirituality, increasing or developing your intuition, using some type of divination, for transcending the physical and trying to communicate with someone telepathically, and in asking for guidance from whomever or whatever you call your higher power. This is the most powerful direction.

SOUTH corresponds to the element of fire. Face south for love issues, relationships of any kind, creative and artistic pursuits, anything of a romantic or emotional nature.

EAST corresponds to the element of air. Face east for career issues, strength, clarity, new business opportunities, financial matters and any endeavor requiring extra energy, healing of the mind, new beginnings.

WEST corresponds to the element of water. Face west for letting go and moving on, increasing self-esteem, forgiving yourself or someone else, cleansing, unconditional love.

Special Note: When in doubt as to which direction to turn, face north, because it is the foundation of all things.

If the compass direction you're using does not put you in view of the Moon, do not be concerned. The energy of the Moon enters from all around you even if your back is to her. Try to face the direction that I suggest in the spells as opposed to facing the Moon itself. The energy coming down from the Moon is all you need to acknowledge.

For the best of both worlds, conduct your spell outside when the Moon is directly overhead or almost overhead. In that way, you can see the Moon from any direction.

Another suggestion is what I often do: Sometimes when I am casting a spell inside, I peak my head out the door for a few seconds to get a glimpse of the Moon to feel the connection and then come back inside and perform my ritual. Relax . . . Moon vibrations can permeate through rooftops, mountains, clouds, rain, snow, and even the apartment of the people above you.

4

Why and How to Perform Spells

To cast a spell is to conduct a ritual. Do we need spells and rituals to get what we want in life or to make things go more smoothly? The answer is no. If you have strong faith and a forceful mind, you can create what you want by merely thinking it is. There is no need of magick tools, incantations, and all the things that accompany casting a spell.

So why do it? There are many reasons. Conducting a ritual is an appeal to our subconscious mind. The act in itself slowly puts us in an altered state or trance that places us in a frame of mind to concentrate better on what we are seeking. It eventually builds up to a crescendo of intention and willpower.

A ritual spell begins by gathering our magickal tools, such as candles, incense, and whatever else is required. The tools or enhancements are symbolic—they work with your subconscious and tell you when to go from the physical world to a world of magick. The moment I pick up my knife I use for rituals (Wiccans would call it an *athame*), I can feel myself moving into a mystical environment. As I place my candles, I feel the energy of the room changing. You must be aware of every feeling and emotion from start to finish. Everything you do in these rituals must have intention behind it, and you must realize that you are creating an enchanted area in which to work your spells.

When you cast a formation, you enter deeper into the subconscious. Each step takes you deeper and deeper, away from the mundane. By the time you recite the incantations for the spells, you are "powered up" to a point of generating great energy and are entirely focused on what you want.

For example, a spell to land a wanted job is a far more powerful choice than someone sitting at home thinking, "Gee, it would be nice if I got that job tomorrow." You are actually sending out vibrations that soar through the cosmos to bring the reality back to you. You are raising energy.

Also, rituals give you something to do that is constructive instead of worrying about things. A lady I knew from Asheville, North Carolina, proved this point. She applied for a loan at a bank that to say the least was a "long shot." It was Friday, and she had to wait until Monday before she would have an answer. She called me on Friday night and said she was pacing, eating too much, and feeling like a nervous wreck. I recommended a spell for her. It took her all day Saturday to gather up the items she needed, and on Sunday afternoon, she performed her spell. Before she knew it, the weekend was over.

Instead of agonizing over her situation, she felt she was doing something to give her loan a better chance of being approved. She was not sure she really believed it would work, but felt it was worth the effort since she could not concentrate on anything else. That in itself was a good reason to conduct the ritual.

Monday afternoon, the phone call came from the loan officer telling her she did get the loan, but only because they decided to give her a special exception. Was it the spell or would it have happened anyway? She commented that whatever it was, the spell certainly did not hurt. Also, if you worry too much and assume failure, you will create it. She rerouted her nervous energy to create what she wanted.

Some people conduct spells just because they're fun. If you are performing spells with a group, it is a great reason to come together and a way of socializing and using creative talents. It is a way for people to bond. Personally, I take spell casting very seriously and do it for more than just fun, but I do not conduct spells often. When you decide you are going to cast a Moon spell, it should be out of true necessity.

Do not cast spells too often. It should be done for special occasions and for special reasons if you really take it seriously.

Learning when to conduct a Moon spell is of the utmost importance, as discussed earlier. Plan well ahead and give yourself all the advantages.

How to Conduct a Spell: The Advance Work

- Decide which spell you will be using. If you're writing your own, do it well before the day of execution in case you decide to change it after thinking about it for a day or two.
- Check to make sure you have all the tools or enhancements available. You do not want to run out to a store an hour before you conduct these rituals. You should be as relaxed as possible the day of your ceremony.
- Locate the area in which you will be casting your formation in advance.
- Choose your clothing and make sure it is clean and ready to wear.
- Clear your schedule so you are not rushed.
- If the spell is to be conducted at home, clean it so you won't be nervous or concerned about chores later.

Moon Spell Day: The Basic Order

1. Shut off all telephones, pagers, and anything that will distract you.
2. Put pets that will disrupt you in another room.
3. Take children to the babysitter's if you have made that previous arrangement, or ask household members not to disturb you for the amount of time you think it will take. Allow a minimum of half an hour.
4. Take a shower or bath.
5. Take your tools and enhancements and go to your spell area. Make sure you have your spell.
6. If you're using music, you may want to start playing it while

you are getting things together.

7. Move furniture around to give yourself the space you require.
8. Place all your tools within the space you will be using.
9. Cast your formation according to above directions and place your candles and gemstones according to the diagrams.
10. Relax and visualize your body being protected by a bright white light. See it flowing from your toes up to the top of your head. Not only does the formation protect you, but the white light is also a shield of additional protection from negative influences.
11. Sit, and when you feel it appropriate, recite your spell. You may want to listen to the music for a while before actually reciting the spell, or you may want to sit in silence to prepare.

The specific directions of the spell will direct you from here. It may be writing something on paper, drinking wine or juice from a chalice, etc.

1. Once you have completed your spell, sit for as long as you feel is comfortable. Extinguish all candles and open up your formation, release it, and leave immediately. (See formation section for how to open up and release a formation.)
2. Remove all enhancements and put things back in order.

5

How to Cast Different Formations

The reason we make a formation of any kind is to center and ground the spell.

It protects and holds the energy in place. Most people chose to cast circles, as there is no beginning and no end, making it strong and effective. It is in and of itself, one.

However, I have found that casting a circle first and then a triangle or a square within it is also powerful and protective for different types of spells. Therefore, I suggest one of the three formations for each individual spell. If you are not at ease with using a triangle or square within a circle, stay with the circle only. Remember, never use a square or triangle alone. Always cast them within your circle.

As I have repeated, these are really your choices, and there is nothing you should force yourself to do if it does not feel right. If you are not sure of what formation is best suited to you, experiment. Let the higher self within guide you. Follow the direction that is given to you. In the spell section of this book, I suggest what formation to cast for each particular spell. However, you can change this. Remember that it is your spell, so do what you will.

Material Items to Cast a Formation

Your objective is to create a circle, triangle, or square in which you alone or you and others can sit. Using material items is a *visible* way to cast a formation. Some people like to physically define a space by the use of something one can see. Salt is an excellent choice as it represents preservation, purification, and enhancement. Nature's gifts like pebbles, seashells, stones, sticks, flowers, and sand make lovely items in which to figure a formation. I have also seen the use of tarot cards, crystals, and candles. If you are performing the ritual inside, you do not want anything that may stain a floor or carpet. When outside, it is helpful to use something that will not blow away. I have a permanent circle of bricks in my meditation garden that I use for ceremonies, and when I work magick, I just invoke the energy, which I will discuss later in this chapter.

Visualization to Cast a Formation

If you do not choose to use any visible materials, you can cast a formation by picturing it and drawing it with an invisible line.

To cast a formation in this manner, use something that extends from your body that you can point, such as a wand, crystal, or knife. In essence, you are using a type of mystical drawing pencil. If you use a knife, it must not be used to cut anything physical and may be used only for ritual reasons. If the thought of a knife, dagger, or sword of any kind is jarring, simply do not use one. Also remember the knife can be dull, as it is used to direct energy only.

I have a friend that uses a beautiful letter opener to cast formations for her spells. Some may laugh, but she does some great magickal work with that letter opener, and she wouldn't give it up for the sword of Sir Lancelot! Try a long crystal, or attach a crystal to the end of a stick or a piece of copper pipe (copper is a conductor) and make your own wand.

If you're not comfortable finding a tool (such as a wand) that can direct energy, then cast your formation with an extended arm. Point your first and second fingers to direct the energy and draw your imaginary formation.

You can also combine methods by casting your circle with visualization and your inside formation with a material element like salt or stones. Or, cast your circle with a physical item and your inner formation with visualization.

There are many different kinds of tools available to help you cast your invisible boundaries. If you have decided to use a tool instead of an outstretched arm, that instrument should be kept in a safe place and a place of dignity. Before you use it, bless it with element water if you like, or let it sit under the light of a full Moon to absorb energy and to be cleansed.

How to Cast a Formation

When you decide what type of commodity you will use to create your formation, be it a circle, triangle, or square, you can begin. Have all of your tools and enhancements you'll need for your spell nearby. Be organized and think before you begin. Once you cast your formation, it is best not to have to leave because you forgot something. If you are sitting on a chair, it should be kept in place. If you are using tools or enhancements, they should be on a table or sitting on the floor in which the formation will eventually be cast.

White Light Protection

Before casting your formation, apply "white light" protection by visualizing a white light of protection around you. The white light will protect you from negativity entering into your body. It may look like a cloud, a tower of light, an oval, or whatever you feel the image to be.

It should encompass your entire being for at least the size of the area that you will use to cast your formation. For example, if you are casting a square that will be approximately 6 feet x 6 feet, your white light shield of protection should be at least 6 feet around your entire body. If a circle is 9 feet and five people are included, your white light protection should emanate 9 feet from each person's body.

To bring forth the white light of protection, stand in your spell area, close your eyes, and visualize the white light coming from above you and flowing down and eventually encompassing you. It enters through the top of your head and streams slowly down to your toes and grows outward from there. It should come to the very edges of your formation. If with others, they should all protect themselves with the white light method.

Drawing the Formation

Next, stand in the direction in which you will be eventually facing to cast the spell. Turn in a clockwise manner, as you will always cast a circle first. Then, also in a clockwise direction, cast your triangle or square. Sprinkle your salt or place your stones or whatever item you have chosen until you have traced a complete formation and are back at the starting point. Do not be concerned if the formation is not perfect. It may have a wave or two, but that is of no concern. One person must be chosen as the caster (person who casts the formation), or facilitator, while the others take their places standing or sitting until the formation is completed. To indicate that the formation is cast and convey to everyone to bring up the energy in the space, an acknowledgment of the completion of the process is recited.

As you say the following words, remain standing and raise your arms with palms up as if lifting the energy up from the earth.

Say "This ________ (fill in circle, triangle, or square) cast with all-knowing eyes, bring forth the power, may the energy rise." If you prefer to shorten this, merely say "May the energy rise."

At this point you can be seated and begin your spell as directed.

Opening and Closing Your Formation If You Need to Leave

If for some reason you must leave your formation before the spell is completed, you must create an invisible doorway in which to leave. Whether you used stones or a wand, you should not leave without the proper passage. If you are using a circle of seashells, for example, stand and take your right hand with your first and second fingers (like a blessing) and pass your hand over the shells at a height that is comfortable for you and large enough for you to fit through.

You have made an invisible door. Step over the shells and leave. Do not step on any item that has made up your formation—always step over it. Once on the other side, immediately close the circle in the same manner. When re-entering, open the circle in the same way and close it again when you are back inside.

This should take only seconds, as it is virtually done with the sweep of an arm.

Although it is not recommended that you leave, things do arise. Sometimes we forget a lighter to light candles or the spell itself. A doorbell can ring, and we have no choice but to answer it. If you are gone for more than ten minutes, however, your area will lose energy and you should start again. Remember that you are part of the energy within the formation, and without you there, it cannot breathe for long. No harm is done if this happens; it just dissipates naturally like wood in a fireplace. Just start a new fire.

Releasing Your Formation When Finished

Everything needs closure when something is completed, and that also applies to formations. When your spell is accomplished, you must release the energy of the formation. To do this, stand and hold your arms up with palms down angled above your shoulder (as if ready to dive into the water), and in a gentle pushing motion, lower your arms and visualize the energy going back down into the earth.

Say, "The energy is released," or other closing words, such as "Done," or "It is."

The Circle

The circle is the most important formation—this is why all other formations are cast within a circle. There is good reason for that—it works! It fulfills all the needs in any spell and achieves what is necessary in a beautiful and transcendent way. It shields and is a place to contact the God of your understanding, the gods/goddesses, the universal life force energy, spirit guides, angels, or any of the ascended masters. It can also be adapted solely for a place to balance and receive messages from spirit or your inner self, having no spells involved. Sometimes I cast a circle for no special reason. I simply sit and relax, not releasing any energy or taking in any energy. I do not give or receive . . . I "just be."

(See the "Spell for Any Purpose" at the end of the book.)

Note: When in doubt as to which formation to cast, cast a circle.

The Circle is representative of: wholeness, universal life force, power, achievement, balance, and emotions.

Solitary placement: Sit directly in the middle of the circle and face the direction suggested in the spell or the direction that is comfortable for you.

Group placement: Always face each other, inward. If only two, face each other. If three, form a triangle inside and decide amongst yourselves who will sit where. Four or more should have one person at each compass point and the rest fill in. Alternate males and females if the numbers allow. No one should sit in the center with his or her back to the others. The facilitator or the group leader should take his or her place with everyone else.

The Triangle

The pyramids are triangular; the body, mind, and spirit are a trinity. Christian religions recognize the "Father, Son, and Holy Spirit." The three phases of the Moon in different belief systems are represented as the three faces of the goddess: "maiden, mother, crone." The maiden is a waxing Moon, the mother a full Moon, and the crone the waning Moon.

We see the power in threes through symbology from ancient culture to modern days. Three is a number of multiplication and abundance.

The ancient Greek mathematician Pythagoras spoke of three as the perfect number . . . a beginning, middle, and end.

In mythology, a group of three associated gods were referred to as a triad.

In daily conversation, we employ our own form of verbal triads using groups of words such as: animal, vegetable, mineral . . . land, air, and sea . . . width, depth, and height . . . and the list goes on and on and on. Three is truly a magickal number and is powerful when working spells.

The Triangle is representative of: self-expression of creative and artistic pursuits, spirituality, power and high energy, psychic abilities, astral projection and divination.

Solitary placement: Sit at the base of the triangle facing the direction suggested in the spell or the direction that is comfortable for you.

Group placement: Always face each other, inward. If two people are present, each should sit at the left and right base of the triangle ,leaving the point open and free. If there are three, each person should take a point of the triangle. If more than three, take the three points and fill in wherever the others are comfortable.

The Square

Buildings have four sides, a table has four legs, and there are four compass points on a map. All fours represent stability. To cast a spell using a square is not as powerful as a circle or triangle. However, when casting for reasons such as work and career, it is the very best. This is a very specific formation. I think of it as the "no nonsense" formation.

If it is love you want, DO NOT use a square. Although the stability of a relationship could possibly fit in, for the most part, a square is all business. A square is an excellent foundation to build upon. For spells that have to do with homebuying or building, the square is the perfect choice. If you want an idea to be set into solid form, this is the formation that should be chosen.

People drawn to a square formation can sometimes tend to be workaholics: very practical, productive, and very organized. So if you tend not to be too successful in life or you are a little on the lazy side, the energy from the square may help to balance you. If you are ambitious, energetic, and hard-working but financially void and "luck" has not been with you, the square is also a good choice.

The Square is representative of: stability, work and career, all business matters, legal issues, money affairs, and organization.

Solitary placement: Sit directly in the middle of the square and face the direction suggested in the spell or the direction that is comfortable for you.

Group placement: Always face each other, inward. If only two, you should face each other, one facing the direction north and the other south. For three, form a triangle within the square. Two sit at the base and the third at the point. For four, each take a compass point, not a corner. For more than four, take the compass points and then fill in, alternating males and females if numbers allow.

Whether you cast a circle, triangle, square, or some formation of your own, if you have done it with belief, true intention, and seriousness, you should feel a difference in energy within that area. You have created a mystical place of your own, a place that is unique to you—a place that no one else can ever claim or copy. If you are with others, your synergistic efforts have created a place that is unrivaled by any other group. It is perfect for you.

6

Moon Spell Checklist

This checklist is provided to help you stay organized as you prepare to perform any of the spells in this book. It will make the process go more smoothly.

Make photocopies of this checklist or use it as a guide to write down what you will require. If you are making copies, I suggest you make extras and keep them in the front or back of the book for future use.

DO NOT WRITE ON THIS PAGE

Checklist

Name of Spell			Page No.
☐	Candles	Number:	Color(s):
☐	Chalice or special glass		
☐	Crystals or gemstones		Type(s):
☐	Element Water		
☐	Fireproof container		
☐	Incense		Type:
☐	Jewelry or talisman		Type:
☐	Knife or wand		
☐	Matches or lighter		
☐	Music		Type:
☐	Paper and pen		
☐	Salt		
☐	Wine or fruit juice		
☐	Miscellaneous items		

• 7 •

Finding Time

Busy work schedules, family commitments, and social activities can make it challenging to find the time to prepare for and perform spells. Sometimes a short amount of time to be alone is the most difficult. If you are single and have a living area to yourself, you should have no problem. However, for the mothers and fathers who have a house full of children and animals, it is quite a different story.

Nighttime is an excellent choice. Perhaps when family members have gone to sleep, you can make the extra effort to awake at a certain hour, such as two o'clock in the morning, to conduct your spell. In the very early morning hours, the energy of the planet is lower as most people are sleeping and chaos is minimal. In fact, studies have shown that we are most psychic at approximately 4:00 A.M. for this very reason. If you tend to awaken from sleep with premonitions or intuitive thoughts in the middle of the night . . . check your clock. There is a good chance it will be around 4:00 A.M.

If arising at an early hour of the morning is not a possibility, then you may have to sacrifice some appointment during the day or evening to perform your spell. For example, if every week you get together with a special friend for lunch or go to your pottery class, you may have to sacrifice the meeting and use the time to spin your magick.

Instead of the half an hour it would take to prepare the family meal, order out or put a frozen dinner into the microwave. Your average spell takes thirty minutes to an hour, depending how elaborate you want to make it and the time you like to just sit and meditate or reflect after the spell is complete. *Do not* rush anything. Spinning a spell is not like rushing into a grocery store, buying groceries, and preparing the quickest meal possible just to put food in your stomach. It is a mystical, magickal, spiritual ceremony in which you may well receive a result far beyond what you ever thought possible. A blessing like this is nothing to rush.

I recently made arrangements to cast a spell with a friend of mine for the following week. Unexpectedly, he came over to my house to drop something off and asked, "While I'm here, can't we just take ten minutes and do that spell?" He did not understand the process at all. You must slowly build up to the day of the spell. The anticipation and the preparation are all part of the process of creating what you want and bringing it to fruition.

Part of the power is the development of energy raising, which starts with the first decision about what type of spell you are going to work.

If you must, hire a baby-sitter or ask a friend to watch your pet or children for a period of time—it is worth the effort. People have taken time off from work to cast a spell.

I am not promising if you miss work, the money lost will come back through the use of a spell; but if you are serious, you will find the time. I have seen people rent motel rooms just to get away by themselves and not be disturbed. Ask a friend if you could use his or her home for an hour or so while they are shopping if you have no other choice.

You will find a way to make the time.

You may not be in a position to shut off telephones and have total silence. If this is the case, you must use the right side of the brain a bit more and utilize your creativity. As mentioned earlier in the chapter "Where to Conduct Your Spells," if the bathroom of your house is the only place in which to be alone, that is what you must do. It is not an insult to the Universe if this is all you have to work with. Sometimes a garage, basement, or attic may be used, unless someone attempts to start looking for you, wondering what you are doing.

8

Overcoming Problems

There are two types of problems that may arise while casting a spell—one is mental and the other is physical. The mental can stem from concerns about your religious beliefs or fear of what other people may think of you. In all religious beliefs, there is some type of ceremony or ritual that is involved. No one is suggesting you leave your religion in order to execute these rites. This is an act to enhance your life. You are neither hurting, nor cheating, nor being blasphemous in my opinion. If a clergyperson tells you this is not the case and you are going against the God of your understanding, it is up to you to make the choice. I believe you are merely venturing down a road that may lead to a process that appeals to your subconscious mind to make things happen.

I have good friends and clients that practice everything from Judaism, to Catholicism, to Buddhism, and they all use spell magick to better their lives. However, they do not stand up on a soapbox in the middle of town and let the world know of their personal practices. They have come to an understanding in their minds and have no guilt or regrets.

That being said, the idea of discussing this with others is up to you, but I do not suggest it if you live among individuals who would scorn such ideas. This is not because these ideas are wrong, but just because some people are afraid of what they do not understand.

The subject of metaphysics is controversial. One of the biggest dilemmas I hear from individuals who conduct spells is being with a partner or family member who does not approve of such activities. Sometimes these people expect you to have the same thoughts that they have and do not want you to experiment or try something different. This is not an easy situation, and I have seen divorces over the practice of metaphysical beliefs. Use common sense, and as they say, "let your conscience be your guide."

Belief systems and approaches to life are personal. No two roads to a destination are found by the same map. Therefore, respect other people's point of view and do not try to convince someone to rethink their convictions and consider your philosophies instead. Be quiet in your soul searching and exploration of different methods that are available to you for creating a successful and fulfilling life. Why make a show of things?

We all have the right to delve into new avenues of interest. If someone around you does not agree, you may want to consider conducting your rituals elsewhere or stay very private in what you do. The important thing is that you do nothing to harm anyone physically, mentally, emotionally, or on a spiritual level.

While I was renting a house in Sedona, Arizona, I met a woman in her seventies who lived down the block. She was a lovely lady, and we became friends in a short time. I told her I was a writer, and she asked what I wrote about. At the time I was writing about the power of prayer and spirituality. I summed up the subject by saying I was writing on spirituality, which, in fact, was the truth. I did not disclose that I was a third-generation psychic and believe in the philosophy of metaphysics.

As we drove past some of the vortexes in Sedona, she began talking about what she described as "New Agers," by which definition I would best be described. I liked her so much, I did not comment or try to defend New Age thought.

I felt it was for the best. What would it have proven and what would it have accomplished? I did not lie; I just chose not to comment one way or the other. One of my better strengths is knowing when to discuss things with certain people and when not to. I do not want someone to attempt to convince me their beliefs are the best, and I do not discuss my beliefs with others unless they ask me and show an interest.

In all cases, be discreet about such sensitive subjects. If you live in a home in which the idea of spinning a spell is looked down upon, show discernment and respect for others. Rise above the situation with class, and show others you are not as judgmental as they may be about you.

If you should start to feel uneasy about spell making, it is not worth sacrificing your peace of mind, and I would recommend stopping it immediately. If you love the idea, the rituals, and the results, continue doing it. Be true to yourself as long as you never hurt or intentionally cause anyone harm. If these spells work well for you, you may want to share them with others of like mind.

The other kind of challenge you may need to overcome when using magick is the physical aspect of making things work. If you are in a very small space and think you cannot cast a circle because a dresser or a bed is in the way, it is not a problem. Cast the formation right over any obstacles. Naturally, you must use the visualization technique of casting a formation as opposed to using material items such as salt. In some areas you may not be able to use candles or other items, but work around it and you will be surprised by what you can achieve.

The weather is always a factor when casting spells outside. One question was addressed to me during a lecture I gave in Kansas City. Can a spell be spun outside in the rain?

My answer? Why not, if there is no lightning about? If you want to sit outside with a gentle rain falling, you may regard it as the element of water entering into your spell with a little extra force. Some may see rain as purification or a cleansing.

For me, to be rained on as I sit in a chair or on the ground trying to concentrate is not conducive to tranquility, and I would rather go inside or reschedule the entire event. This is a personal preference. The rule of thumb you may want to remember is, if something is a distraction and takes away from your concentration, you are putting undo stress on yourself. So why do it?

Regarding pets: Not everyone has a separate room to put a pet into when doing a ritual. You may not feel it is right to lock your pet up while performing these actions. Sometimes the animal will protest with scratching or barking or whatever your pet does when upset. If you have a pet that is quiet and will sit calmly and you feel you want this peaceful creature to be a part of your ritual, then include her. For the most part, if it is easier to have the animal next to you than wandering back and forth, in and out of your formation, have him in the formation.

Can you use your beloved animal to take the place of a person, hence having a group ritual? Not really, unless it understands what the ceremony is about and can also concentrate on the same intention.

9

Creating and Walking a Moon Circle

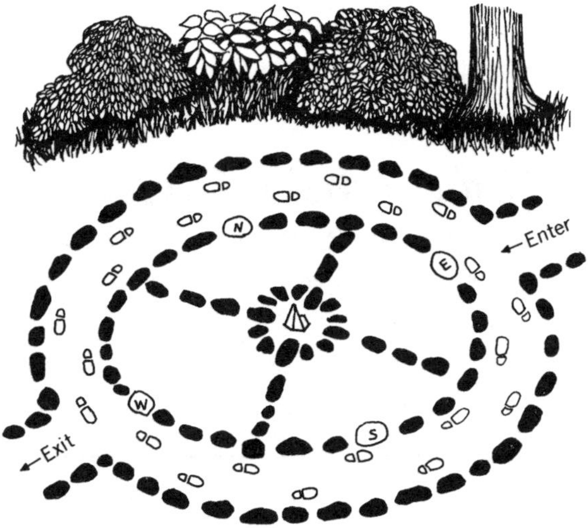

A Moon circle is a place to receive messages about your future. You can build one for yourself or with others. It is a circle created by the use of shells, rocks, stones, bricks, pinecones, or anything you choose. The reason a circle is used is that the energy comes up faster within a circle and continues to turn, creating a vibration that will allow you to tap into your future more readily. The circle is divided into the four major compass directions, each one having specific meanings and insights.

The Moon circle provides a place sincere people can resolve problems and come to a better understanding of situations, as well as foreseeing future events. With a Moon circle, you can draw from the universal life force energy to receive messages and to prevent disharmony from coming into your life. It is like a magick mirror that looks into the future.

Native American traditions show us the use of a medicine wheel, which has some basic similarities but is far different. I have great respect for the medicine wheel and feel it is a powerful tool for healing and balance. However, the two should not be confused—the medicine wheel is more complex and requires much more understanding of Native American beliefs.

How to Make a Moon Circle

You can style a temporary circle or assemble a permanent one if you live on a piece of land that is spacious. If you have the capability to make your circle outside among nature, you will receive that extra-earth connection. However, if you do not have that opportunity, you can create one in your living room or another appropriate indoor space.

Choose the spot where you will create your circle. It can be an area that just "feels good" to you. You will mark off the four compass points—north, south, east, and west—with some type of stone or indicator. Next, make a second small circle in the center that will surround your crystal, stone, etc. The center circle is the energy point. You may opt to create a third, and largest, circle that encompasses the two inner circles. This provides a walkway around the inner circle, keeping the energy contained. As indicated in the illustration on page 47, remember to leave a gateway or opening from the east through which you enter and one in the west through which you exit.

If forming the minimum temporary-style Moon circle, you will need five stones, crystals, shells, bricks, or whatever you have available to mark the spot.

First place a stone at each compass point and one in the center. Although this may look like a cross, you must visualize an etheric circle connecting the outer stones.

Keep in mind the size of your circle. If you will be working your magick alone, a small circle will do. If you intend to work with someone else or others, you will have to make the circle large enough to accommodate all those involved. Also consider how you will sit. Not all of us are able to bend or move freely. Be practical by placing chairs, stools, or pillows to sit on within the circle before you start your ceremony, if necessary. I use large logs on occasion when outdoors.

How to Walk the Moon Circle

Once your circle is in place, enter the circle from the east, as this is where the Sun rises and is the direction that opens all passages. You will exit through the west, where the Sun sets. If using a three-circle layout, you will have already created an entry point to pass through.

Next you should cleanse yourself and the circle. You may want to use a smudge stick of white sage as a form of purification. You can buy a stick of white sage at most health food stores or New Age gift stores. Light the sage stick and let it smother. When it starts to smoke, pass it back and forth in front of and around your own body as a form of purging. You are bathing yourself in smoke. If others are involved, smudge them as well, passing the smoke around them.

Some people use loose sage and light it in a seashell, using a feather to spread the smoke. However, the sage stick is usually the easiest, as it requires no other tools. Next, smudge the circle in the same manner, spreading smoke throughout the circle to release negativity.

If you do not have sage or prefer not to smudge, simply pass your hand in a sweeping motion over the circle and visualize any remaining negativity leaving the circle. To cleanse yourself, shake your hands in front of yourself as if shooing the negativity away and out of your body. This is the quick and simple way. I do recommend using the smudge stick if possible.

Now you are ready to walk the circle. Start from the east and walk around clockwise at least three times. It will take a cycle of three to bring up the energy of the circle, as three is a number of multiplication. If, after three walks, you do not feel the energy in the circle shifting, continue to walk until you feel it is time to stop.

If others are with you, they should follow. When you stop, stop in the direction you are led to and sit in that section of the circle.

When working with others, they may not choose the same direction to stop or they may want to continue to walk until they are led to their special place. Someone may choose to sit in the same direction with you, as this is where they are led, and others may sit in an opposite place. There is no right or wrong. Sharing a space with someone will not take away energy from you or deplete the messages you are receiving.

You may sit with your hands in a receiving position with palms up, or you may decide to cross your hands and concentrate in a contained manner. Some people feel when meditating or becoming in tune with the universal forces, it is not good to cross hands or legs. I have done both and think that your comfort is the most important issue because you need to be relaxed and comfortable for this particular ritual.

Always sit facing inward, toward the center power point. In other words, you may be in the section that is considered north, but once in the north area, you are actually turned and facing south. The message you pick up will be of a southern nature with crossovers of energy from the north. It is not necessary to know what direction you have ended up in, as you can determine that later.

Once you are seated in your direction or message point, calm your mind and relax. Allow the message to come to you. Ask silent questions if you like, and see what answers you intuit. Once you feel you have received your messages or answers from the collective consciousness, take your time and slowly rise.

Give thanks to the energy of the circle by saying something to yourself or out loud such as, "I give thanks to the earth and the life force for guidance." Make up what you like. You may just say a simple thank-you with a bow of the head. Acknowledge the power from above that has visited to help and guide you. Leave the circle from the west, where the Sun goes down, as this gives closure to the ceremony.

Meanings of the Four Directions

North

From the north springs forth wisdom and completion. It is a time of delivery and freedom from things that may have been a challenge in our lives. It is a call for balance in all things. Its message is to find answers here and now using practical solutions and common sense.

As we travel upward, moving in a northerly direction, our journey may become more difficult as we are nearing the end of a cycle. It is this direction that instructs us that this is not the time to give up when we are so close to completion. This direction can have difficulties attached to it, but the trip will be well worth the result.

Here is where things are concluded and you may feel the most equalized. North represents power, organizing, insight, and justice. Whenever in doubt, turn north.

South

Everything emotional comes from the south. Symbolically, south is a time for preparing for the future. It is a place of emotion and affairs of the heart. This point represents passion and fullness and reminds us to learn to control our bodies. Here we learn self-control of our emotional selves and how to express feelings without hurting others. It is in the south that we also learn to release feelings of hurt and anger.

Creativity stems from the south as well, and we can make the connection to artistic pursuits and issues dealing with imagination and inventiveness.

East

The day begins in the east. It is renewal, birth, and rebirth. It is with this direction that we find spontaneity, innocence, hope, and trust. The first light enters from the east, providing leadership and guidance. We learn many lessons from the messages of the east. We learn to believe in what we cannot see, feel, or touch. We learn to be more open-minded to things we do not understand. This is a place where a new venture or a different path through life may be awakened.

It is also from this direction we must recognize that in order to proceed into the future, we must accept and deal with the present. Once we have accomplished this, we can move in a different direction. This is the conception of all things, including love, career, health, spirituality, and balance. You may have already been through many of life's tests. But when spirit moves you to try yet again or venture out to do something new, you will find yourself in the direction of the east.

West

The Sun sets in the west and brings in the night, mystery, and dreams; it is the gateway to the unknown. The direction west signifies completion of a situation or goal.

It can suggest to you that it is time to complete something you have been procrastinating about. Power and strength generate in the west. This compass point prescribes determination and development. The west tells us to go within ourselves for guidance where the energy is calmer and your level of tension sets like the Sun. We find acceptance of who we are; and if we don't like what we find, we must change it.

If you are not looking for a specific message or answer within a Moon circle but feel you need the connection to a specific direction, walk your circle and intentionally sit in the direction from which you feel you need to draw guidance and absorb its energy through meditation. Example: If you do not know whether to interview for a new job, sit in the direction east and concentrate.

Be careful of meditating too much in the northern compass point, because like the winter, you may lose your warmth. Use all directions in moderation.

PART II

Creating a Magickal Atmosphere

Introduction

Nothing is more important to a successful spell than creating the right atmosphere and the kind of mood that will be both inspirational and relaxing. Some of these enhancement ideas and magickal tools are necessary as an integral part of the spell, while others are optional. Each spell states whether something is optional or not. Don't feel you have to try all these ideas at once—experiment.

• 10 •

Magickal Enhancements

Food and Beverage

Three simple words: Keep it light! A spell on a full stomach is not recommended. A heavy meal can leave you sleepy or uncomfortable. Avoid meat the day of your spell, if you can. Stick with fruits and vegetables as much as possible. Fish—baked, but not fried or in a heavy sauce—is a good option. Wait at least two hours after eating to begin your spell.

Try to avoid caffeinated or carbonated beverages; distilled water is an excellent choice because the impurities have been removed. A cup of caffeine-free herbal tea is soothing and relaxing. Try a blend of chamomile and passionflower. Although some of the spells include a sip of wine or fruit juice during the actual spell, do not take it to extremes.

Clothing

As with food and drink, here, too, three simple words apply: natural, loose, and clean. One hundred percent cotton is a wise choice. A loose white gauze garment is nonrestricting and gives you a sense of cleanliness and purity. Some individuals enjoy taking the time to find certain color garments for special spells. The same colors listed in the candle color chart (see page 63) can be used for clothing as well.

If you do not have a cotton garment, choose something as close as possible, like a cotton blend. Comfort is important: Tight jeans and belts do not allow your body to relax. However, wear jeans if they are the most comfortable thing you own—and most jeans are 100 percent cotton. If you are in a private place, you may decide to just wear a robe, towel, or oversized T-shirt. You may even opt for nudity. The choice is yours.

Before you get dressed, make every effort to take a bath or shower. Start fresh and clean. Think as you are showering or bathing that you are washing any negative energy off your body. A bath is an excellent idea, especially if you use music and candlelight.

If you're doing a group spell, bathe or shower before leaving the house or before the group arrives. If you can't shower, at least wash your hands and face. If you can wash your feet, that's even better. If water is not available, shake your hands and visualize negativity being removed.

Music

Music has the ability to create a sense of peace—providing it's the right music.

By virtue of the fact you are reading this book, I feel safe in saying you most likely are a seeker of peace and well-being. In all likelihood, you already have in your possession music that soothes you. Slow classical music or New Age music seems to be the most popular. Drumming and chanting recordings are also something to consider. Nature tapes offering gentle background music can be found in most department or music stores.

After purchasing any new tape or CD, listen to the entire recording before using it for spell work. The first two selections may be ideal, but if song number three goes up thirty decibels and a wolf starts howling, it could send you crashing down from your altered state.

If you have the time, visit your local music or New Age store. Most provide headsets and demonstration tapes that give you the opportunity to listen before you buy. The recording you choose should be long enough to last your entire spell.

Music that suddenly stops in the middle of a ceremony will also break the mood. If you have no choice and you must turn a tape over, at the very least have your sound system close to you so you do not have to leave your spell area. Music is the sound of the soul: If you can include it in your rituals, all the better.

11

Magickal Tools

Any tangible item used for ritual can be considered a magickal tool as long as it means something special to you. The creative part of our brain works in symbols, so it makes sense to use symbols as a way to conduct creative magick. You probably already have magickal tools and may not even recognize them. It may be your favorite picture that makes you "feel good" upon merely looking at it, that special coin that a relative gave you when you were a child, or a favorite pen you've had for years.

Candles

Candles bring light into our lives—both literally and symbolically. They chase away the darkness and allow new projects, thoughts, and relationships to emerge. Lighting candles before a spell can create very powerful energy.

Candles also represent the three levels in which we exist. The wax corresponds to our physical body, the wick to our mind, and the flame to our soul or spirit.

Candles come in a myriad of colors, shapes, and sizes. Some are scented, some unscented. For our purposes, shape and scent (or lack thereof) are unimportant. Do give some consideration to the size of your candle. If you deem your spell will take an hour, don't light a candle that burns for only thirty minutes.

Color is a significant part of what candle burning is all about. Different colors represent different vibrations. As the candle burns, the vibration of that color is released. Refer to the color chart to clarify which color best suits your needs. You may use just one candle or a combination.

If you don't have the ideal color available, use white. When burning a white candle, pay attention to the smoke. When it starts to smoke, negative energy is being cleansed from the area. When the smoke subsides, the energy in that area is cleansed and clear.

Take caution in purchasing a white candle that is too inexpensive. Inexpensive white candles smoke too readily and can confuse you. However, I would also not advise going to the extreme and looking for top-of-the-line candles. Use common sense and buy moderately. When working with candles, always use caution and do not leave them unattended.

Candle Color Interpretation

Candle Color	Associated Energy
WHITE	Purity, power, newness, spells, healing, peace, and psychic skills. White will intensify the effect of any color candle it is used with.
BLACK	Removal of negative energy; not a color of evil or negativity. Release and banish.
BLUE	Peace, tranquility, protection, fidelity, astral projection.
BROWN	Protection for the household; telepathy, stability.
SILVER	Neutralizer of negative energy or forces.
GREEN	Prosperity, money, success; counteracts jealousy, ambition.
ORANGE	Provides additional energy needed for work or other endeavors; promotes order, control over the self.
PINK	Love, friendship, romance, affection, giving.
PURPLE	Intuition, psychic pursuits, power and independence, wisdom.
RED	Fertility, physical strength, sexual passion, courage.
YELLOW	Well-being, self-esteem, attraction, glamour, action.

As mentioned earlier, this chart can also be used as a guide for making clothing color choices.

Incense and Fragrances

In my experience, people either love incense or they have an aversion to it.

Incense also comes in different sizes, shapes, and forms. Some types of incense are already labeled with names reflecting the effects they hope to achieve: There is stress-relieving incense, energy incense, love incense, and so on.

Some people prefer to burn potpourri or oils. One of the purposes of incense in these particular rituals is to bring you into an altered state of consciousness in the most peaceful way possible. If the smell of sage or sandalwood calms you, use it. But if your sinuses say no, give them respect.

Don't get caught up in what others have decided is the best aroma for you. For example, studies have shown citrus fragrances promote energy, and the smell of lilac can calm us. But don't force yourself to inhale a scent you don't care for simply because the label states "incense for romance." Always buy what you enjoy.

Experimenting with new aromas is also fun. Most incense is inexpensive and sometimes sold by the stick. One thing to be careful of: If you are going to do a spell inside or in a small area, try your new purchase out prior to its actual use. Otherwise, you may be subject to a disagreeable smell for hours, if not days. Incense can take a while to dissipate and may linger in the air for a long period of time.

Here are some recommended scents and herbs you may want to try that correspond to certain magickal work. Remember: These are only suggestions and not a must.

Health

Bay
Carnation
Cedar
Eucalyptus
Juniper
Lavender
Lemon Balm
Myrrh
Pine
Sage
Sandalwood
Thyme

Love

Apple
Musk
Rose
Ambergris
Basil
Cinnamon
Chamomile
Dragon's Blood
Jasmine
Lemongrass
Patchouli
Peppermint

Career/Job

Vanilla
Allspice
Clove
Nutmeg
Pine
Wisteria
Heliotrope
Spruce
Sage
Mint
Honeysuckle
Cedar
Bayberry

Women's Issues

Musk
Orange
Hyacinth
Myrrh
Pine
Rose

Men's Issues

Musk
Cedar
Jasmine

Spirituality

Frankincense
Heliotrope
Jasmine
Sweetgrass
Gardenia
Pine
Sage
Violet
Sandalwood
Rose

Crystals and Gemstones

Crystals bring life to our quartz watches. They receive and transmit radio waves. Without quartz crystals, the computer age would never have happened: They are what make up integrated circuits and electronic chips.

The power of crystals go far beyond the products we have derived from them. They are important tools in magick, having the ability to focus and direct energy to a specific intention. Some say they have healing powers, mentally, physically, and spiritually.

Many other stones also have special energies that can assist in your spells. For a quick reference, I've listed a few below. But this is a huge area of exploration. If you want to know more, your local bookstore or library will certainly contain numerous books on the subject.

Gem Stone Qualities

A special note about quartz crystals: These stones are available in nature stores, gem shops, and most New Age gift stores in rough or polished form. You need not spend more than a few dollars on your crystals. Start with something small, and go to a larger size if you feel it's necessary. If you are unsure of which is the best stone to intensify your spells, use a clear quartz crystal.

Clear quartz crystal—stimulates healing, balances the elements to fulfill us and make us whole. Aids psychic development.

Amethyst—a very powerful spell stone. Psychics and healers have used its curative properties for years. Helpful in dispelling anger and anxiety, aids in feeling less scattered.

Carnelian—often called the stone of good luck. Said to purify the blood, stimulate sexual emotions, and aid in sexual function.

Lapis lazuli—draws love to us. It is also reputed to be effective in healing headaches, high blood pressure, depression, insomnia, and other such ailments.

Malachite—increases energy, is connected to change and creativeness. The Egyptians wore crushed malachite as eye shadow to guard against the evil eye.

Moonstone—is said to be a stone of magic. It increases psychic abilities and is used widely for spell rituals. Astral projection is accelerated when using a moonstone.

Rose quartz—also known as the love stone. A stone that deals with the energy of all the emotions.

Turquoise—builds strength, provides protection. It is the sacred stone to the Native Americans. It is a protective stone for horses and their riders. In Arabia it is a stone of meditation. It has the quality of absorbing negative energy.

When purchasing, carefully touch the crystals at the store. A stone chooses you, you don't choose it. It will just "feel good" to you, having something the others don't possess. Use your gut feeling—which is your intuition talking to you.

Charging Your Crystal

Once you find your crystal, it needs to be "cleared, charged, and programmed." Cleanse it of a past owner's energy and/or the energy that has been placed on it by individuals examining it by washing it in cold water or letting it sit in a bowl of water.

Next, use the Moon to charge your crystal. Place it overnight in view of one of the phases listed below:

New Moon—a crystal charged in this phase specifically offers energy that supports new beginnings, confidence, hope, and specifically anything of increase.

Full Moon—a crystal charged in this phase brings power to support anything you want to achieve. This is actually the best all-around phase to utilize.

Once you have cleared and charged your crystal, the last step is to program it. Hold it in your hand, and focus on the vibrational energy you are looking for to accomplish your goal. Visualize your final goal, but not the way you think you're going to get there.

For example: If you want to lose twenty pounds, see yourself on the scale twenty pounds thinner. Don't try to analyze the way it will come about. This is best left to your higher power to solve.

If you choose, you can program any of your other gemstones as well.

Element Water

Throughout the spells you will see the use of what I refer to as *element water.* Element water is basically water that has been charged to help you do magick during a thunderstorm.

It represents fire, earth, air, and water, a forceful mix of elements at their highest potency. Lightning represents fire, which corresponds to power, energy, magick, and lust. Thunder represents air, which corresponds to spirituality, health, and knowledge. The strength of the storm represents earth, which corresponds to nature, being grounded, wisdom, and all things material. The rain in itself represents water, which corresponds to emotions, reflection, love, creativity, and purification.

How to Make Element Water

Basically you are collecting rainwater with intention. First you will need a container to collect the water. I have used glass, plastic, clay pottery, and almost any type of container one can use, and I have seen no difference. You may feel a natural material is better or something you feel is special has more impact. If these are your thoughts, then seek a special container. I personally use two or three chalices.

The important thing is that the container is new or extremely clean, having been sterilized in a dishwasher or by boiling if it is made of glass. If the container is new, still clean it to remove energies from other people who may have handled it. Because thunderstorms are not all that common, I recommend obtaining as much water as possible so you will always have some on hand.

If you know that a storm is approaching, take your container and place it in a spot where it will collect water. Some people always leave a container outside just in case, and others only place one out when they are almost certain a storm is near.

After the storm and your water has been collected, you should invoke a "hand blessing." Place both hands above the container with your palms facing down and say, "Bless this water. May it empower my intentions."

Now, transfer your element water into a practical container for later use if you are not using it immediately. A glass or plastic jug or bottle with a lid is a good choice.

This water is not limited to use only during rituals. It can also be used to bless something. Feel free to separate your water into smaller bottles for traveling or even to give a small bottle to a friend. It is a perfect gift for someone who is like-minded because it comes from nature and you have put your personal energy into it with good thoughts and well wishes.

Around the holidays, I take element water and put it in tiny plastic containers with little labels that read, "Element Water." I then tie ribbons around the necks of the containers and give them to special friends in case they want to bless something. I used element water to bless my car, computer, office, home, and the cat next door!

See "Element Water Blessings" under the section on miscellaneous spells in this book for a short but powerful blessing ceremony.

Special Notes

- Element water will only be powerful when rain, lightning, and thunder are all present. An average rain will not do.
- Do not use water that flows from a gutter! It may seem to be a very easy solution, especially if you want a large amount quickly. However, the fact is the rainwater being channeled through the gutter is not as pure as water coming directly from the sky because it has picked up debris.
- Do not be concerned about pollution in the air when gathering water. Your blessing over the water purifies it.
- Do not drink the water, as it is not meant for your inner body.
- If you are not in an area where you are able to collect water, ask a friend to do it for you. However, you must conduct the "hand blessing" once it is in your possession.
- Be cautious in thunderstorms and do not go out when lighting is about. For safety reasons, wait till the storm is over to bring your collected water inside.

Additional Magickal Tools

Other magickal tools that I mention in Part III on spells will include the following. Feel free to substitute what is available or what works for you.

Wand or knife: Sword, athame, letter opener, or any type of wand or long crystal. Any pointed object that extends as a pointer will work. One can purchase decorative wands displaying gemstones and crystals in New Age gift stores, fantasy stores, or through Internet Web sites. A double-edged knife is also available through the same sources.

Fire-burning container: Iron pot, mini-chiminera (small Mexican fireplace), ashtray, metal trash can, cauldron. Anything that can contain a piece of paper being burned within a safe vessel.

Special drinking glass: Any container that can hold wine or grape juice: wine glass, cup, bowl, chalice, or favorite goblet.

Optional tools:

- Flowers and fruit
- Religious statues or holy cards
- Tarot cards or Runes (or other methods for telling future events; psychic forms of divination)
- Pendulum (Information on making decisions using a pendulum can be found in Chapter 18.)
- Pentacle or pentagram symbol (The pentacle is a five-pointed star with lines connecting with a circle encompassing it. A pentagram is the same five-pointed star but has no circle. This symbol represents the elements earth, air, fire, water, and what is sometimes known as the fifth element, spirit. A pentacle or pentagram can also represent the human body with legs and arms outstretched. This symbol is often used in rituals as a form of protection while the ritual is underway. The star should always be in an upright position. The reverse is considered to be negative.)

- Cross—any kind (The universal symbol of a cross represents the bringing together of multiple dualities into a single whole. It can represent human form with extended arms, as well as a crossroads in your life. Crosses have numerous religious and spiritual meanings.)
- Bells (A bell can be rung to invoke universal powers and note the beginning of a ritual. Some people use bells as a form of protection to keep evil away.)

Who knows what contains magick and love for each individual? But I do know if you have such items, you should hold them dear and use them to assist you.

Personal Altars

To have a personal altar is by no means a requirement for doing spell work, but it is an excellent place in which to keep your magick tools and to worship whomever you choose. Use it not only as storage for these special items but also as a place to pray, meditate, and to receive answers from your higher self.

An altar can be any area that is flat. It can be a separate small table or any section on your dresser. The top of a large sound speaker could be used; a bookshelf or two cement blocks with a piece of wood laid across them would do. Once again, you get to be creative.

You may not want to have a permanent altar but prefer to set up a temporary one just for your spell use. Your altar typically would display items such as candles, incense, wands, knives, gemstones, statues, chalices, element or holy water, and anything else that you would use as a special component that had spiritual and enchanting properties. I do not feel there is any special way to set up an altar. Move things around until it looks and feels right to you.

An outside altar is also a lovely thing to create if possible. It can be built near a favorite tree using stones and bricks. You may construct a special table outside made of wood. To make it even easier, use a tree stump or a rock that is fairly level.

When fashioning an altar, try to stay away from the use of too much metal. Natural materials are always the best. However, if your only choice is an altar containing a lot of metal, try to cover it. Use a natural fabric or put a piece of wood over it. Try to keep things natural.

As for the direction to face your altar, there are many schools of thought. Some suggest facing north because it is the most grounded direction. Others will recommend facing the altar east because it is the direction the Sun and Moon rise. Each direction has its special meaning and place. Therefore, I feel you should put it anywhere in which it is practical.

I have seen rolling altars, where people have made altars on the top of units that have wheels so they can roll through a room to face the direction they feel it needs to face for a particular spell or meditation. A rolling altar can also be kept out of the way in a closet if you are pressed for space.

Altars are extremely personal, as well as very interesting, and there is no right or wrong way in which to set up this area of sacred items.

PART III
Spells

Introduction

As a magickal practitioner, you should consider these spells with a great sense of seriousness. If you are confronted by troubling issues and these rites resolve them, then I have attained my purpose in sharing this material. Remember that your intentions must be for good and harm no one or yourself on any level. These ceremonial magick techniques are intended for use in addition to common sense and logical efforts to achieve your desires. Be patient, as you are appealing to invisible forces to help you acquire visible results. If, after several efforts, you still do not reach the objective you are looking for, accept that the universe has something better in mind for you. At the very least, you have been recognized; this attention will promote positive and distinguished movement in your life.

12

Health

When one door of Happiness closes, another opens, but we often look so long at the closed door that we do not see the one which has opened for us.

—Helen Keller

A good health spell can do wonders for the psyche. However, none of these rituals is intended to replace traditional medical or psychological treatment. These spells are intended to be considered an addition to any necessary treatment or remedies health care professionals may suggest.

The mind is instrumental in the healing of the physical body and rituals are a request to the subconscious, as well as to the body itself, to restore any disease it may have.

When a distinct idea gets its direction from mental focus through concentration and determination, we have the ability to make an entrance into a unique and effective realm—one from which healing and positive transformation are available to us. Performing a healing spell or ritual serves as petition to the universal life force for assistance.

When such a spell does work, the possibilities may be nothing less than phenomenal. You do have the ability to control your body and your mind. The challenge is to consider new avenues and explore areas that may be different from what you have previously experienced.

Continued Good Health

Necessary Enhancements and Magickal Tools

The necessary tools for this spell include any tools you have chosen for your formation as described below.

You will need:

- element water—rainwater that was charged in a storm where there is both lightning and thunder. (See Chapter 11 for instructions on how to gather element water.)
- small bowl

Candles

You will also need a **blue** candle, a **red** candle, and a **white** candle. Set the candles in front of you in a row with the blue to the left, white in the middle, and red to the right.

Formation

All spells should begin with casting a circle, which is your shield of protection. If you are using a triangle or a square, cast your circle first and then cast your formation within it.

The best formation for this spell is the **circle.**

Cast your formation using methods described in Chapter 5 of the book using a wand, a knife, an extended arm with fingers pointed, salt, or other materials you may have chosen.

Direction to Face

This spell is most effective if you are facing **north.** Arrange your candles and any tools or enhancements that will be in your formation so that they will be in front of you when you are sitting facing north.

Moon Phase

This spell will work best if cast during the **waxing phase** of the Moon because we are hoping to increase good health just as the Moon is increasing as it waxes.

Day of the Week

This spell can be cast on **any day** of the week.

Optional Magickal Enhancements

The following items will add a deeper dimension to your spell and help you to focus yourself more fully, but they are not necessary, and the spell can be cast even if you don't have these items available.

Gemstones

The best gemstones to use for this spell are **clear quartz crystal** and **amethyst.** If using additional gemstones other than those recommended in your formation, place them in front of you.

Incense

Incense that will enhance this spell would be **lemon balm** or **thyme.** Place incense in a safe place within your formation if you like. However, starting the incense outside of your formation is fine if you want to enjoy the aroma while organizing your spell work.

Music

If you like music and will not find it distracting, you might want something **New Age, meditative,** or **classical;** think soothing and harmonious for balanced health. Whatever you are comfortable with will be best.

Before You Start Your Spell

Make sure you have no distractions.

Turn phones off if possible.

Play soothing music.

Keep the lights dim.

Wash your hands or shower before you begin.

Light incense if you are using it.

Gather everything you need and have it close at hand.

Draw your formation.

Ask your higher power to allow the information to flow through you.

Affirmation

Affirmation to be read within your formation *before you actually begin your spell.*

I take nothing for granted, especially my health. I have everything when my body, mind, and spirit all are in harmony. I am encircled by a healthy and healing aura. May this excellent state of health that I now experience continue. I am appreciative and give thanks to my higher power for focusing this energy to me.

AND SO IT IS.

How to Perform the Spell

Dip your fingers into your element water and touch your chest and say, "My body is sound."

Dip your fingers back into the element water, touch your forehead, and say, "My mind is stable."

Lastly, dip your fingers back into the element water, touch the top of your head, and say, "My spirit is good."

Conclude with any statement that signifies closure of the ceremony in your mind such as, "And so it is," "Blessed be," or "Amen." Now extinguish your candles and release your formation by visualizing it lifting off the ground, up through the roof, into the sky, and finally into space, where it disappears.

When the ceremony is complete, pour the remaining element water on a plant or outdoors if possible. Do not save the remainder. If you cannot throw it outside, gently pour it down the sink, pass your hand over the drain, and say, "Back to the earth."

Controlling Anger

Allow extra time for this particular spell as it takes some writing time.

Necessary Enhancements and Magickal Tools

The necessary tools for this spell include any tools you have chosen for your formation as described below.

You will need:

- paper
- a pen or pencil

- matches or lighter
- fire-burning container

Candles

You will need a **black** candle, or you can use three candles: **black, blue,** and **silver/gray.** Set the candle(s) in front of you, either just the black candle centered or three in a row with the blue to the left, black in the middle, and silver/gray to the right.

Formation

All spells should begin with casting a circle, which is your shield of protection. If you are using a triangle or a square, cast your circle first and then cast your formation within it.

The best formation for this spell is the **circle.** Cast your formation using methods described in Chapter 5 of the book using a wand, a knife, an extended arm with fingers pointed, salt, or other material items you may have chosen.

Direction to Face

This spell is most effective if you are facing **west.** Arrange your candles and any tools or enhancements that will be in your formation so that they will be in front of you when you are sitting facing west.

Moon Phase

This spell will work best if cast during the **waning** or **dark phase** of the Moon because we are hoping to decrease anger just as the Moon is decreasing as it wanes.

Day of the Week

Cast this spell on **any day** of the week with the exceptions of Wednesday and Thursday, when it would be less favorable.

Optional Magickal Enhancements

The following items will add a deeper dimension to your spell and help you to focus yourself more fully, but they are not necessary and the spell can be cast even if you don't have these items available.

Gemstones

The best gemstones to use for this spell are **tiger's eye** and **obsidian.** If using additional gemstones other than those recommended in your formation, place them in front of you.

Incense

Incense that will enhance this spell would be **pine** or **bay.** Place incense in a safe place within your formation if you like; however, start the incense outside of your formation.

Music

If you like music and will not find it distracting, you might want to play something **New Age, meditative,** or **classical;** think soothing and harmonious for calming inner turmoil.

Before You Start Your Spell

Make sure you have no distractions.
Turn phones off if possible.
Play soothing music.
Keep the lights dim.
Wash your hands or shower before you begin.
Light incense if you are using it.
Gather everything you need and have it close at hand.
Draw your formation.
Ask your higher power to allow the information to flow through you.

Affirmation

Affirmation to be read within your formation *before you actually begin your spell.*

I release my anger about (name the person or event). Anger does not benefit me. My anger is a choice that I will not choose anymore. Anger poisons my system. I recognize when I get angry it's caused by frustration and not understanding why someone does not think or act like I do. I now realize it is not fair to choose anger because someone does not think like me. Give me the insight to accept that I cannot own someone else's behavior. I will not allow someone else's behavior to make me unhappy.

The next time I become angry, bring forth the reminder to me that anger is a choice. I will then try breathing deeply for a few seconds and postpone my anger. The time after that, I will postpone it even longer, lengthening the time. Eventually, I will realize I can control this anger. I will feel a sense of accomplishment and pride. I will be stronger; and with this new self-control, I will be able to accomplish anything. Surround me with this vibration.

AND SO IT IS.

How to Perform the Spell

First, light your candles, then take your paper and pen and write a brief letter to the person or situation you are angry with. If you are angry with yourself . . . write to yourself.

If you are angry with someone who is dead . . . still write. If you are angry with an event that happened that caused you pain, write to that event. If you are angry about an object that hurt you or someone . . . write to it.

If you do not care to write letters, simply write a few words to get the point across. Example: Rick, I am angry you left me for a job in

Boston. Illness, I am angry you made me have surgery when I had no medical insurance.

If you have no problem writing a lengthier letter, tell him, her, or it how you feel and why you are angry with them. Be very honest and go into detail. No one will ever actually see the letter; it is your secret letter. In fact, if you are going to really expound, you may want to sit at a table or desk and type it or write it before you go into your spell area. The reasoning behind this letter writing is that it puts your thoughts into physical form, removing them from your subconscious.

Next, take your letter or note and burn it in your container. If a little bit is left, that is okay, as long as you cannot make out any special words or people's names.

If for some reason you do not want to burn it, you can always tear it into the smallest pieces of paper you can and set in water so it is really destroyed. Then throw it away later. A great many people have felt new beginnings after this ritual, as this is a freeing release.

After you have burned your note, say the following incantation:

Today I made a forceful choice,
To start to live, hence I rejoice.
My anger leaving, blessings be,
I am revived, I am set free.

Conclude with any statement that signifies closure of the ceremony in your mind, such as "And so it is," "Blessed be," or "Amen." Now extinguish your candles and release your formation.

Releasing Addiction

If possible, eat no meat, chicken, or fish on the day you plan to cast this spell. Meat can weigh you down—you need to feel light so you can open the doors of your psyche more easily to remove and release your intention. Also, to eat meat is to have a dead animal inside you, and you want as few negatives as possible.

Necessary Enhancements and Magickal Tools

The necessary tools for this spell include any tools you have chosen for your formation as described below.

You will need:

- scissors
- piece of black string, rope, cord, ribbon, yarn, or anything that can be easily cut. If you cannot find something black, any color will do.
- a bowl filled with cold water
- a small quartz crystal gemstone

Candles

You will also need candles—**silver/gray** to the left, **white** in the middle, and **black** on the right—set in a row in front of you.

Formation

All spells should begin with casting a circle, which is your shield of protection. If you are using a triangle or a square, cast your circle first and then cast your formation within it.

The best formation for this spell is the **circle.**

Cast your formation using methods described in Chapter 5 using a wand, a knife, an extended arm with fingers pointed, salt, or other material items you may have chosen.

Direction to Face

This spell is most effective if you are facing **east.** Arrange your candles and any tools or enhancements that will be in your formation so that they will be in front of you when you are sitting facing east.

Moon Phase

This spell will work best if cast during the **waning** or **dark phase** of the Moon because you are hoping to release and decrease a compulsion just as the Moon is decreasing and disappearing as it wanes.

Day of the Week

Cast this spell on Sunday, Friday, or Saturday, with **Sunday** being the most favorable.

Optional Magickal Enhancements

The following items will add a deeper dimension to your spell and help you to focus yourself more fully, but they are not necessary and the spell can be cast even if you don't have these items available.

Gemstones

The best gemstone to use for this spell is **chrysolite.** If using additional gemstones other than those recommended in your formation, place them in front of you.

Incense

Incense that will enhance this spell would be **honeysuckle.** Place incense in a safe place within your formation if you like; however, start the incense outside of your formation.

Music

If you like music and will not find it distracting, you might want to play something peaceful and slow in low frequencies like **piano** or **flute.** Whatever you are comfortable with will be best.

Before You Start Your Spell

Make sure you have no distractions.

Turn phones off if possible.

Play soothing music.

Keep the lights dim.

Wash your hands or shower before you begin.

Light incense if you are using it.

Gather everything you need and have it close at hand.

Draw your formation.

Ask your higher power to allow the information to flow through you.

Affirmation

Affirmation to be read within your formation *before you actually begin your spell.*

On this day I've chosen to finally make a change in my life. I do this not because of anyone's influence, but because I do not like this part of me. The time has come because I say it's time. It was part of my evolution in life. I have been there and learned this is not how I want to spend my entire life. As the Moon provides me with the positive strength and energy I need, and my higher power is my witness: I release my addiction to (state addiction).

I release the need to know all the answers I continue to ask myself about this excessive behavior. At this stage in my life, I open myself to positive change. I will separate myself from people and situations that will tempt me to continue in the manner I have in the past. I know when I use my addiction for fulfillment, I will feel a void.

I am excited with the idea that where the universe sees a void, it will be filled with a positive. What will that new positive influence be? I recognize it is three times three better than my addiction. It will not be addictive, it will bring me happiness and pride. I will not try to guess what this gift is, but I know it comes closer and closer as my addiction gets farther and farther away. If I am unable to completely help myself, I will have the presence of mine to seek professional help from others who have dealt with this before.

My very intention today, with this powerful Moon above, has already started the flow of energy to reduce this excessive behavior and unwise risk. The next time I feel the need to (state addiction), I will look to this guide, whether day or night, rain or shine, and remember if I stray, it will take me that much longer to receive that beautiful gift the universe is sending me.

I release my addiction to: (state addiction). (Repeat three times.)

How to Perform the Spell

1. Take your cord and tie a knot in it. This knot is your addiction that has kept you bound.
2. Look at the knot and think of all the hardship and problems this addiction has caused you and others. Reflect for a while if you choose.
3. When you feel ready, take your scissors and cut the string, leaving the knot hanging at one end. It does not matter if you cut to the left or right of the knot, but do not cut the knot in the middle.
4. Take the string, place it in your envelope, and seal it.

5. Shake your hands three consecutive times away from your body as if you were shaking the addiction off of yourself.

Now say the following incantation:

I find more strength here every day,
My will is gaining so I say,
Take this concern, it now unbound,
I am released, my soul is found.

Conclude with any statement that signifies closure of the ceremony in your mind such as "And so it is," "Blessed be," or "Amen." Now extinguish your candles and release your formation.

Once you release your formation, dispose of the envelope containing the broken cord in any manner you choose. Toss it in the garbage or fireplace, bury it, or cast it into the sea.

Releasing Fear

If possible, eat no meat on the day you plan to cast this spell.

Necessary Enhancements and Magickal Tools

The necessary tools for this spell include any tools you have chosen for your formation as described below.

You will need:

- a knife
- large pin
- pen, or something that can be used to carve a letter or word into a candle

Candles

You will need a **black** or **blue** candle centered in front of you.

Formation

All spells should begin with casting a circle, which is your shield of protection. If you are using a triangle or a square, cast your circle first and then cast your formation within it.

The best formation for this spell is the **circle.**

Cast your formation using methods described in Chapter 5 of the book using a wand, a knife, an extended arm with fingers pointed, salt, or other material items you may have chosen.

Direction to Face

This spell is most effective if you are facing **west.** Arrange your candles and any tools or enhancements that will be in your formation so that they will be in front of you when you are sitting facing west.

Moon Phase

This spell will work best if cast during the **waning** or **dark phase** of the Moon because we are hoping to release and decrease a fear just as the Moon is decreasing and disappearing as it wanes.

Day of the Week

Cast this spell on Sunday, Friday, or Saturday, but **Sunday** being the most favorable.

Optional Magickal Enhancements

The following items will add a deeper dimension to your spell and help you to focus yourself more fully, but they are not necessary, and the spell can be cast even if you don't have these items available.

Gemstones

The best gemstone to use for this spell is **aquamarine.** If using additional gemstones other than those recommended in your formation; place them in front of you.

Incense

Incense that will enhance this spell would be **rosemary** or **lilac.** Place incense in a safe place within your formation if you like; however, start the incense outside of your formation.

Music

If you like music and will not find it distracting, you might want to play something peaceful and slow like piano, flute, or acoustic guitar. Whatever you are comfortable with will be best.

Before You Start Your Spell

Make sure you have no distractions.
Turn phones off if possible.
Play soothing music.
Keep the lights dim.
Wash your hands or shower before you begin.
Light incense if you are using it.
Gather everything you need and have it close at hand.
Draw your formation.
Ask your higher power to allow the information to flow through you.

Affirmation

Affirmation to be read within your formation *before you actually begin your spell.*

Today I am choosing tranquility over fear. I know the issue is not whether I am capable of controlling my feelings of fear, but will I choose to. How much will I suffer before I make a choice? The choice is now, and it is for relaxation and well-being. Situations, people, things, places, or animals do not make me fearful. I cause this emotion. I know I have more control than I am aware of. I will work at being less fearful and know I am in control.

AND SO IT IS.

How to Perform the Spell

Hold your black or blue candle. (Black is for banishing and blue is for healing; and as we are banishing *and* healing, either color will work nicely.)

On the top of your candle around the wick, carve the word or just the first letter of the fear you are trying to release. For example, if you are trying to overcome a fear of flying, carve the letter F or write the entire word.

Light the candle and wait until the wax melts down around the letter or word until you can no longer see it. (Note: Do not carve on the sides of the candle; use the top.)

As you are waiting for the wax to cover the letter, say the following incantation:

The candle burns, so does my fear,
To the divine I ask you hear.
Protect me from this constant dread,
This spell is done and all is said!

Conclude with any statement that signifies closure of the ceremony in your mind such as "And so it is," "Blessed be," or "Amen." Now extinguish your candles and release your formation.

Tarash—A Special Form of Healing

Tarash is a method of healing I have developed for myself and some of my clients. It is a visualization technique that appeals to our subconscious mind. It has personally worked for me and numerous others that have ventured to try it.

The name was derived from the combination of the two words *tar* and *ash.* The principle is that any illness or *dis-ease* in your body should be visualized as black tar. This can include depression, excess weight, or whatever you physically or mentally desire to withdraw from your being. You see the tar leaving the body and slowly it turns into what looks like ash, as the color becomes lighter and lighter from the original tar color.

Eventually the ash becomes even more faint in color and still lighter until you see only white light running through your body as you are cleansed of what was poisoning your system. To you it may even look like a clogged water pipe that starts to push black, dark, murky water through until it eventually runs only clear water.

Note: This method is intended to enhance, not replace conventional or alternative healing methods. I do not intend for it to be used as a prescription or treatment of any kind.

Necessary Enhancements and Magickal Tools

The necessary tools for this spell include any tools you have chosen for your formation as described on the next page.

Candles

You will need a **black** candle placed on your right and a **white** candle placed on your left.

Formation

All spells should begin with casting a circle, which is your shield of protection. If you are using a triangle or a square, cast your circle first and then cast your formation within it.

The best formation for this spell is the **circle.** Cast your formation using methods described in Chapter 5 of the book using a wand, a knife, an extended arm with fingers pointed, salt, or other material items you may have chosen.

Direction to Face

This spell is most effective if you are facing **north.** Arrange your candles and any tools or enhancements that will be in your formation so that they will be in front of you when you are sitting facing north.

Moon Phase

This spell will work best if cast during the **waning** or **dark phase** of the Moon.

Day of the Week

The most favorable day of the week to cast this spell would be on **Monday** or **Saturday.**

Optional Magickal Enhancements

The following items will add a deeper dimension to your spell and help you to focus yourself more fully, but they are not necessary and the spell can be cast even if you don't have these items available.

Gemstones

The best gemstone to use for this spell is **clear quartz crystal**. If using additional gemstones other than those recommended in your formation, place them in front of you.

Do not use any incense during this spell.

Music

If you like music and will not find it distracting, you might want to play **something that signifies healing** to you. Music with background vocals would be okay with this spell—Enya, for example. Whatever you are comfortable with will be best.

Before You Start Your Tarash Spell

Make sure you have no distractions.

Turn phones off if possible.

Play soothing music.

Keep the lights dim.

Wash your hands or shower before you begin.

Light incense if you are using it.

Gather everything you need and have it close at hand.

Draw your formation.

Now is the time to light the candles.

Ask your higher power to allow the information to flow through you.

How to Prepare for Tarash Healing Spell

1. Before you begin or even cast your circle, visualize the diseased area in your body: See the dis-ease as black tar. If you are not sure where on your body your concern is, then just see your entire body as filled with black tar. You must locate this negative matter before starting the spell.

2. Decide where on your body a release point will be. Your release point is similar to a hatch, hole, tube, drain, or whatever image you're comfortable with. The idea behind this visualization is that you will be releasing the poisonous tar through this point.

   Use your own ideas and do what feels best. As an example, it may be thought of like a covered pot filled with steam. Once you remove the cover, the steam rises upward. Here we have the same concept. You must allow an opening in your body somewhere for the negativity to release.
3. When the process is completed, you must close the release point. Decide what will be the best way for you to close the area. For example, see a hatch coming down, a cover being put back on, or something being closed by the motion of your own hand, the hand of an angel, God of your understanding, or whatever you feel suits the situation.

Once you have these thoughts clear in your mind, you can begin the actual spell.

Beginning the Tarash Healing Spell

1. Become very still in your meditation area and keep your eyes closed. Breathe deeply in and out for a few minutes. When you feel relaxed, visualize the opening of your release area. Envision black tar being released from your body in a slow stream. Give this some time; it is not a quick process. See the tar traveling through your body to your release point. Let it flow out at its own speed.
2. Eventually the black tar will turn to an ash color. This means the dis-ease in your body is lightening, but not completely gone. The ash will become lighter and lighter. See it leaving.

As the ash leaves your release point, see the place in your body that is being cleared. Fill it with white light. The white light enters and fills the areas where the tar originally had been. When all of the ash is out of your body, you'll start to see white light filtering out. This means you are filled with clean energy and can now close the release area anytime you choose.

3. Rest for a while in your meditation area after you close the release point. Say "I give thanks, and so it is."

Note: The amount of time it takes depends on how much of a problem you have. It can take several sessions before you even start to see any ash. On the other hand, for lesser concerns, you can be clear in one session. Your intuition will let you know.

When you are finished, extinguish your candles and release your circle formation.

Well-Being and Happiness for Others

Necessary Enhancements and Magickal Tools

The necessary tools for this spell include any tools you have chosen for your formation as described below.

You will need:

- element water
- a bowl or glass for water
- effigy—a representation of the person, like a photograph or

something that belongs to them or that they have touched such as a business card or necklace. If you do not have anything that represents them, write their first and last name on a piece of paper or make something that represents them like a cloth or stick doll. You can also use a clear quartz crystal as a representation.

Candles

You will also need four candles set in a row in front of you: **purple** to the left, **white** next, then **brown** and **pink** to the right.

Formation

All spells should begin with casting a circle, which is your shield of protection. If you are using a triangle or a square, cast your circle first and then cast your formation within it.

The best formation for this spell is the **circle.** Cast your formation using methods described in Chapter 5 of the book using a wand, a knife, an extended arm with fingers pointed, salt, or other material items you may have chosen.

Direction to Face

This spell is most effective if you are facing **north**. Arrange your candles as stated above and any tools or enhancements that will be in your formation so that they will be in front of you when you are sitting facing north.

Moon Phase

This spell will work best if cast during the **new** or **waxing phase** of the Moon because you are trying to increase something as the Moon increases to fullness.

Day of the Week

Cast this spell on **any day** of the week.

Optional Magickal Enhancements

The following items will add a deeper dimension to your spell and help you to focus yourself more fully, but they are not necessary and the spell can be cast even if you don't have these items available.

Gemstones

The best gemstones to use for this spell are **rose quartz, moonstone,** and **topaz.** If using additional gemstones other than those recommended in your formation, place them in front of you.

Incense

Incense that will enhance this spell would be **chamomile, gardenia,** and **peppermint.** Place incense in a safe place within your formation if you like; however, start the incense outside of your formation.

Music

If you like music and will not find it distracting, you might want to play something instrumental that is **light and uplifting.** Whatever you are comfortable with will be best.

Before You Start Your Spell

Make sure you have no distractions.
Turn phones off if possible.
Play soothing music.
Keep the lights dim.
Wash your hands or shower before you begin.
Light incense if you are using it.
Gather everything you need and have it close at hand.
Draw your formation.
Ask your higher power to allow the information to flow through you.

Affirmation

Affirmation to be read within your formation *before you actually begin your spell.*

May (person's name) maintain a safe path and may happiness engulf (her/him). May (person's name) course in life be joyous and fulfilling. Wherever you are, whatever you are doing, may you sense this loving energy I am sending to you through the light of the universe. I unite with you when you pray or ask for divine help even if you are not aware. Every time you think of me, for only a brief moment, I am with you.

AND SO IT IS.

How to Perform the Spell

Take your effigy of the person you are sending positive thoughts to and set it in front of you. Place your hand on top of it and recite the following incantation:

Through all the universal power,
Feel my presence there this hour,
I wish you peace and wish you cheer,
Feel me, see me, I am here.

Take element water and sprinkle it on the effigy.

Conclude with any statement that signifies closure of the ceremony in your mind such as "And so it is," "Blessed be," or "Amen." Now extinguish your candles and release your formation.

Dispose of the remainder of the element water by throwing it on a plant or outside. If you must dispose of it down the sink, pour it gently and pass your hand over the drain and say "back to the earth."

Do what you will with the effigy. There is no right or wrong as it has already served its purpose.

13

Love

Wedding or Partnership

This is a love-binding spell between two people in the most positive way.

Anyone in a romantic partnership can perform this spell. You can perform it as often as you like as a renewal of a commitment you made to each other or for the beginning of a commitment you have both decided to make.

Necessary Enhancements and Magickal Tools

The necessary tools for this spell include any tools you have chosen for your formation as described below.

You will need:

- one chalice or wine glass
- wine or juice (red only), representing the mixing of blood
- lavender oil
- small scissors, like mustache or nail scissors
- envelope
- two pieces of ribbon, rope, or yarn (red or white), or black leather cords, approximately 6 inches long—a size that will fit around each individual's wrist. Leather bracelets work as well, if you can find them.

Candles

You will also need a **pink** candle, a **white** candle, and a **red** candle.

Formation

All spells should begin with casting a circle, which is your shield of protection. If you are using a triangle or a square, cast your circle first and then cast your formation within it.

The best formation for this spell is the **circle,** with you and your partner in the circle facing each other, one to the north and one to the south. Cast your formation using methods described in Chapter 5 of the book using a wand, a knife, an extended arm with fingers pointed, salt, or other material items you may have chosen.

Direction to Face

This spell is most effective if you are **facing each other,** one to the **south** and one to the **north.** Arrange your candles to your right on one side, and put any tools or enhancements that will be in your formation in a place that is comfortable for you.

Moon Phase

This spell will work best if cast during the **full, new,** or **waxing phase** of the Moon because we are hoping to increase love and bring it to fullness, just as the Moon is increasing as it waxes to full.

Day of the Week

The most favorable days of the week to cast this spell would be on **Monday, Tuesday, Thursday, Friday,** and **Saturday.**

Optional Magickal Enhancements

The following items will add a deeper dimension to your spell and help you to focus yourself more fully, but they are not necessary and the spell can be cast even if you don't have these items available.

Gemstones

The best gemstone to use for this spell is **rose quartz.** If using additional gemstones other than those recommended in your formation, place them in front of you.

Incense

Incense that will enhance this spell would be **patchouli, cinnamon,** and **jasmine.** Place incense in a safe place within your formation if you like; however, start the incense outside of your formation.

Music

If you like music and will not find it distracting, you might want to play something instrumental that you find **romantic** or **soothing.** Whatever you are comfortable with will be best.

Before You Start Your Spell

Make sure you have no distractions.

Turn phones off if possible.

Play soothing music.

Keep the lights dim.

Wash your hands or shower before you begin.

Light incense if you are using it.

Gather everything you need and have it close at hand.

Draw your formation.

Ask your higher power to allow the information to flow through you.

Affirmation

Affirmation to be read within your formation *before you actually begin your spell.*

Today we choose to make a vow that we will love and respect each other through all things good and trying. We will bind our love under the power of this Moon and be committed to creating a loving and understanding union.

How to Perform the Spell

1. Sit facing each other, one facing north and the other facing south. It does not matter who is facing what direction. The person facing north takes the first sip of wine and says, "May you never thirst."

   He or she passes it to his/her partner and that person sips from the same glass and says, "May you never thirst."
2. Both people anoint each candle with the lavender oil, starting at the base and continuing up to the top of the candles until all the candles are anointed.
3. The person facing south now takes a sip of wine and says, "You are my light."

   The other person does and says the same, "You are my light."
4. Cut a very small piece of hair from each other and place the hair from each person in an envelope together. (Set it to the side.)
5. The person facing north takes a sip of wine and says, "We are one," and the other follows suit as before.
6. Tie the string or cord around your partner's wrist. It does not matter who does this first. The person facing south takes a sip of wine and says, "You are bound to me."

   The other person does the same.
7. Kiss each other and recite the following incantation together:

   We bind our love here tonight.
8. Each removes a few pieces of hair from the envelope and tosses it to the wind. If you don't have enough to throw, just touch a few pieces that will stick to your fingers and shake your hands to the skies.

Conclude with any statement that signifies closure of the ceremony in your mind such as "And so it is," "Blessed be," or "Amen." Now extinguish your candles and release your formation.

Attracting a Lover

This spell is typically cast if you are looking to share intimate moments on occasion with someone but not necessarily looking for a long-term partnership.

Necessary Enhancements and Magickal Tools

The necessary tools for this spell include any tools you have chosen for your formation as described below.

You will need:

- two figures of people cut out of cardboard the best you can (One will represent you and the other the gender of the person you are looking for.)
- patchouli oil
- paper and pen
- a pink envelope

Candles

You will also need a **yellow** candle placed in front of you to the left and a **pink** candle placed in front of you to the right.

Formation

All spells should begin with casting a circle, which is your shield of protection. If you are using a triangle or a square, cast your circle first and then cast your formation within it.

The best formation for this spell is the **circle.** Cast your formation using methods described in Chapter 5 of the book using a wand, a knife, an extended arm with fingers pointed, salt, or other material items you may have chosen.

Direction to Face

This spell is most effective if you are facing **south.** Arrange your candles and any tools or enhancements that will be in your formation so that they will be in front of you when you are sitting facing south.

Moon Phase

This spell will work best if cast during the **full** or **waxing phase** of the Moon because you are hoping to increase (bring to fullness) love opportunities just as the Moon is increasing as it waxes to full.

Day of the Week

The most favorable day of the week to cast this spell would be on **Friday,** but this spell can be cast on any day of the week with the exception of Wednesday and Saturday, when it would be less favorable.

Optional Magickal Enhancements

The following items will add a deeper dimension to your spell and help you to focus yourself more fully, but they are not necessary and the spell can be cast even if you don't have these items available.

Gemstones

The best gemstones to use for this spell are **rose quartz** and **pink tourmaline.** If using additional gemstones other than those recommended in your formation, place them in front of you.

Incense

Incense that will enhance this spell would be **musk** and **ambergris.** Place incense in a safe place within your formation if you like; however, start the incense outside of your formation.

Music

If you like music and will not find it distracting, you might want to play something **soothing** or **sensual,** like Native American drumming, flute, or maybe "Bolero" by Ravel. Whatever you are comfortable with will be best.

Before You Start Your Spell

Make sure you have no distractions.

Turn phones off if possible.

Play soothing music.

Keep the lights dim.

Wash your hands or shower before you begin.

Light incense if you are using it.

Gather everything you need and have it close at hand.

Draw your formation.

Light your candles.

Ask your higher power to allow the information to flow through you.

Affirmation

Affirmation to be read within your formation *before you actually begin your spell.*

At this time in my life I have no desire for a permanent relationship, yet I would like the intimate companionship of someone that is like-minded. I know we will come together for a period of time that will be special; and when the end comes, we will go our separate ways in friendship and in understanding.

AND SO IT IS.

How to Perform the Spell

Once you cast your circle, take the cardboard figures and dab each one with patchouli oil and place them at opposite directions—one at the north and one at the south. It does not matter in which direction a specific figure is placed. Use your intuition for placement.

Now say the following incantation:

Everyday I draw you near,
Until one day you will be here.
Our time is short and has an end,
We both will know and not pretend.
So come you fast and come you sweet,
I cast this spell so we shall meet!

Conclude with any statement that signifies closure of the ceremony in your mind such as "And so it is," "Blessed be," or "Amen." Release your circle, put out your candles, and put your cardboard figures at different ends of a room you choose.

Within the next nine days, continue to move them closer together in any manner you see fit. On the ninth day, put the two figures together and put them in an envelope. You can tie a string or ribbon around them. Do something to keep the two pieces touching. Do not staple them. Keep the envelope near your bed until this person comes into your life. With the eventual end of the relationship, burn the figures and you are both free once more.

Soul Mate

Use this spell to conjure up a like-minded individual that you are attracted to on all levels: physically, mentally, and spiritually. Remember no one person is perfect or has everything we want. You must be patient and do not have any particular person in mind. Let the universe surprise you.

Necessary Enhancements and Magickal Tools

The necessary tools for this spell include any tools you have chosen for your formation as described below.

You will need:

- two rose thorns (These represent a flower of love with the understanding that sometimes when acquiring something beautiful, we may encounter something that is a bit jabbing, such as the waiting in itself. Have extra thorns on hand in case they break when trying to affix them to the candle.)

Candles

You will also need a **pink** candle.

Formation

All spells should begin with casting a circle, which is your shield of protection. If you are using a triangle or a square, cast your circle first and then cast your formation within it.

The best formation for this spell is the **circle.** Cast your formation using methods described in Chapter 5 of the book using a wand, a knife, an extended arm with fingers pointed, salt, or other material items you may have chosen.

Direction to Face

This spell is most effective if you are facing **south.** Arrange your candles and any tools or enhancements that will be in your formation so that they will be in front of you when you are sitting facing south.

Moon Phase

This spell will work best if cast during the **full** or **new phase** of the Moon.

Day of the Week

The most favorable days of the week to cast this spell would be on **Sunday, Tuesday,** and **Friday.**

Optional Magickal Enhancements

The following items will add a deeper dimension to your spell and help you to focus yourself more fully, but they are not necessary and the spell can be cast even if you don't have these items available.

Gemstones

The best gemstones to use for this spell are **rose quartz** and **pink tourmaline.** If using additional gemstones other than those recommended in your formation, place them in front of you.

Incense

Incense that will enhance this spell would be **apple blossom** and **patchouli.** Place incense in a safe place within your formation if you like; however, start the incense outside of your formation.

Music

If you like music and will not find it distracting, you might want to play something **New Age, classical,** or **baroque,** or anything you might find romantic that is instrumental, perhaps with harp or flute. Whatever you are comfortable with will be best.

Before You Start Your Spell

Make sure you have no distractions.

Turn phones off if possible.

Play soothing music.

Keep the lights dim.

Wash your hands or shower before you begin.

Light incense if you are using it.

Gather everything you need and have it close at hand.

Draw your formation.

Ask your higher power to allow the information to flow through you.

Affirmation

Affirmation to be read within your formation *before you actually begin your spell.*

I understand that I must be patient in matters of true love. The forces do not work according to my time frame but according to what is best for me. I also understand that if someone comes along and I assume it is my soul mate, I will take the time to see if this individual is indeed the one I have been looking for. If not, I will not try to force a relationship that is not flowing, and I will move on with dignity and new hope.

Tack your two rose thorns into the center of your pink candle and light the candle.

Now say the following incantation:

I look to the Moon,
I look to the Sun,
Together we will be as one.
I'll wait every day through cold and through heat,
Until we're together, until our lips meet.

Conclude with any statement that signifies closure of the ceremony in your mind such as "And so it is," "Blessed be," or "Amen." Now extinguish your candles and release your formation.

I Can Feel You, Where Are You?

This is a spell to help you make a past life connection.

Necessary Enhancements and Magickal Tools

The necessary tools for this spell include any tools you have chosen for your formation as described below.

You will need:

- wine or juice (white or red)
- chalice or special cup
- a small piece of polished or rough rose quartz

Candles

You will also need **red, yellow, white,** and **pink** candles to be lit after the spell is underway, placed in a row in front of you.

Formation

All spells should begin with casting a circle, which is your shield of protection. If you are using a triangle or a square, cast your circle first and then cast your formation within it.

The best formation for this spell is the **triangle.** Cast your formation using methods described in Chapter 5 of the book using a wand, a knife, an extended arm with fingers pointed, salt, or other material items you may have chosen.

Direction to Face

This spell is most effective if you are facing **north.** Arrange your candles and any tools or enhancements that will be in your formation so that they will be in front of you when you are sitting facing north.

Moon Phase

This spell will work best if cast during the **full phase** of the Moon because we are hoping to increase your opportunity of finding that person you sense is out there for you.

Day of the Week

The most favorable days of the week to cast this spell would be on **Monday, Tuesday,** and **Friday,** but this spell can be cast on any day of the week.

Optional Magickal Enhancements

The following items will add a deeper dimension to your spell and help you to focus yourself more fully, but they are not necessary and the spell can be cast even if you don't have these items available.

Gemstones

The best gemstones to use for this spell are **carnelian** and **lapis lazuli.** If using additional gemstones other than those recommended in your formation, place them in front of you.

Incense

Incense that will enhance this spell would be **musk** and **dragon's blood.** Place incense in a safe place within your formation if you like; however, start the incense outside of your formation.

Music

If you like music and will not find it distracting, you might want to play something **soothing** or **sensual,** like Native American drumming, flute, chanting, or something instrumental you find romantic. Whatever you are comfortable with will be best.

Before You Start Your Spell

Make sure you have no distractions.
Turn phones off if possible.
Play soothing music.
Keep the lights dim.
Wash your hands or shower before you begin.
Light incense if you are using it.
Gather everything you need and have it close at hand.
Draw your formation.
Ask your higher power to allow the information to flow through you.

Affirmation

Affirmation to be read within your formation *before you actually begin your spell.*

Hear the whispers of this Moon tonight. I sense you but do not know who you are or where you are. My mind travels to thoughts of you. Are we destined to be together, or is what I am feeling a part of a past life that once was and is no more? Are you a mere fantasy or do you really exist? Oh, Moon's energy, feel my dismay. Why does this lingering thought of a person I have never met intrigue me so? What holds us back from finding each other? Through grace, if this be my love, then keep us apart no longer.

How to Perform the Spell

1. Light the yellow candle and say: "I am here, come to me."
2. Take a sip of your wine.
3. Light the red candle and say: "Feel me breathe."
4. Light the white candle and say: "May we have light to find each other."
5. Take your rose quartz and pass it over and above the flame of the three candles, high enough so you do not burn yourself.
6. Now hold the rose quartz on your heart and close your eyes. Try to picture a silhouette of someone but not a face. If no vision comes to mind, do not force it. Let it go for now.

Finally light the pink candle and recite this incantation:

I gaze at the Moon with her magickal power,
Are you gazing too, at exactly this hour?
I do not know you, nor words we have spoken,
This spell is now cast and cannot be broken.

Conclude with any statement that signifies closure of the ceremony in your mind such as "And so it is," "Blessed be," or "Amen." Now extinguish your candles and release your formation.

After you leave your circle, take your rose quartz and put it somewhere you will see it daily, if possible. The next time you see another piece of rose quartz, buy it and keep it out of sight. Know that someday you will give it to the person you are meant to be with. And eventually the two gemstones will sit side by side.

Leaving Someone

This may assist you in finding the strength to move forward toward a new life.

Necessary Enhancements and Magickal Tools

The necessary tools for this spell include any tools you have chosen for your formation as described below.

Candles

You will need a **black** candle placed in front of you and a fire-burning container, along with matches or a lighter.

Formation

All spells should begin with casting a circle, which is your shield of protection. If you are using a triangle or a square, cast your circle first and then cast your formation within it.

The best formation for this spell is the **circle,** but for this spell you will be casting your circle counterclockwise instead of clockwise, as you are in essence going backward to a time when this person was not in your life. Cast your formation using methods described in Chapter 5 of the book using a wand, a knife, an extended arm with fingers pointed, salt, or other material items you may have chosen.

Direction to Face

This spell is most effective if you are facing **north.** Arrange your candles and any tools or enhancements that will be in your formation so that they will be in front of you when you are sitting facing north.

Moon Phase

This spell will work best if cast during the **waning** or **dark phase** of the Moon because we are hoping to increase love opportunities just as the Moon is increasing as it waxes to full.

Day of the Week

The most favorable days of the week to cast this spell would be on **Sunday** and **Saturday,** but this spell can be cast on any day of the week.

Optional Magickal Enhancements

The following items will add a deeper dimension to your spell and help you to focus yourself more fully, but they are not necessary and the spell can be cast even if you don't have these items available.

Gemstones

The best gemstones to use for this spell are any black stone such as **onyx, obsidian,** or **jet.** If you are using additional gemstones other than those recommended in your formation, place them in front of you.

Incense

Incense that will enhance this spell would be **lavender, cedar,** and **citrus.** Place incense in a safe place within your formation if you like; however, start the incense outside of your formation.

Music

If you like music and will not find it distracting, you might want to play something with **chanting, drumming,** or **gentle chord patterns**. Whatever you are comfortable with will be best.

Before You Start Your Spell

Make sure you have no distractions.
Turn phones off if possible.
Play soothing music.
Keep the lights dim.
Wash your hands or shower before you begin.
Light incense if you are using it.
Gather everything you need and have it close at hand.
Draw your formation.
Ask your higher power to allow the information to flow through you.

Affirmation

Affirmation to be read within your formation *before you actually begin your spell.*

Within this place where I am, I now look for answers. I feel the wisdom of my guides and my inner self. I sense the presence of the source from which all life comes. I am becoming weary as to the road I should travel. I (have love or have had love) for (person's name), but I feel the demise of what once was a powerful union. Help me overcome my weakness to make this choice to follow it through. I have contemplated the idea of leaving with logic and clarity. I will mourn these circumstances and then move on with new hope and enthusiasm. This situation has been another step of my evolution and was something I was meant to experience. As this door closes, I will not look at the closed door too long, but will look ahead for the one that is opening.

AND SO IT IS.

Stare into your black candle and visualize the person you are leaving becoming smaller and smaller and vanishing within the flame.

How to Perform the Spell

Recite the following incantation:

I wish you well as we now part,
I follow what is in my heart.
Each must walk our separate way,
Our union over on this day.

Conclude with any statement that signifies closure of the ceremony in your mind such as "And so it is," "Blessed be," or "Amen." Now extinguish your candles and release your formation.

Sensual Desire

This spell will give an already existing relationship a bit of a magickal spark.

Necessary Enhancements and Magickal Tools

The necessary tools for this spell include any tools you have chosen for your formation as described below.

You will need:

- red glitter (representing excitement and shimmering passion)
- patchouli oil
- vanilla

(You may want to have a piece of cardboard or a protective surface if working on the floor so the glitter does not stick to carpeting once the spell is finished.)

Candles

You will also need two **red** candles placed in front of you.

Formation

All spells should begin with casting a circle, which is your shield of protection. If you are using a triangle or a square, cast your circle first and then cast your formation within it.

The best formation for this spell is the **circle**. Cast your formation using methods described in Chapter 5 of the book using a wand, a knife, an extended arm with fingers pointed, salt, or other material items you may have chosen.

Direction to Face

This spell is most effective if you are facing **south.** Arrange your candles and any tools or enhancements that will be in your formation so that they will be in front of you when you are sitting facing south.

Moon Phase

This spell will work best if cast during the **full** or **waxing phase** of the Moon because we are hoping to increase love opportunities just as the Moon is increasing as it waxes to full.

Day of the Week

The most favorable days of the week to cast this spell would be on **Monday, Tuesday, Thursday,** and **Friday,** but this spell can be cast on any day of the week with the exception of Wednesday and Saturday, when it would be less favorable.

Optional Magickal Enhancements

The following items will add a deeper dimension to your spell and help you to focus yourself more fully, but they are not necessary and the spell can be cast even if you don't have these items available.

Gemstones

The best gemstones to use for this spell are **carnelian, rose quartz,** and **malachite.** If you use additional gemstones, other than those recommended in your formation, place them in front of you.

Incense

Incense that will enhance this spell would be **apple, ambergris,** and **jasmine.** Place incense in a safe place within your formation if you like; however, start the incense outside of your formation.

Music

If you like music and will not find it distracting, you might want to play something instrumental that is **romantic** and **sensual,** possibly with crescendos. Whatever you are comfortable with will be best.

Before You Start Your Spell

Make sure you have no distractions.
Turn phones off if possible.
Play soothing music.
Keep the lights dim.
Wash your hands or shower before you begin.
Light incense if you are using it.
Gather everything you need and have it close at hand.
Draw your formation.
Ask your higher power to allow the information to flow through you.

Affirmation

Affirmation to be read within your formation *before you actually begin your spell.*

We all have human needs to be more physically passionate at times, and today I will take the initiative to bring more excitement into my life with my partner. I will also consider other physical differences I can make, such as wearing more seductive clothing the next time I am with my partner and creating an atmosphere of romance and intrigue.

How to Perform the Spell

Before lighting your candles, anoint them with the patchouli oil and the vanilla. Start at the base of the candle and work up, dabbing them lightly with the oils as many times as you feel inclined to do so.

Sprinkle a small amount of glitter over your candles (you don't need much).

Light the candles, and recite the following incantation:

May your passion gleam at the thought of me,
May it heighten and grow three times three.
When you look at me feel the fire,
We will soothe that deep desire.

Conclude with any statement that signifies closure of the ceremony in your mind such as "And so it is," "Blessed be," or "Amen." Now extinguish your candles and release your formation.

14

Career/Job

Starting Your Own Business

Necessary Enhancements and Magickal Tools

The necessary tools for this spell include any tools you have chosen for your formation as described below.

You will need:

- an envelope
- a pen
- three small seeds—like poppy seeds or grass seeds

Candles

You will also need **two white** and **two green** candles. Place them on the four sides of the square, not in the corners. You will want a white one in front of you facing east, a green candle on both the north and south sides, and a white candle behind you to the west.

Formation

All spells should begin with casting a circle, which is your shield of protection. If you are using a triangle or a square, cast your circle first and then cast your formation within it.

The best formation for this spell is the **square.** Cast your formation using methods described in Chapter 5 of the book using a wand, a knife, an extended arm with fingers pointed, salt, or other material items you may have chosen.

Direction to Face

This spell is most effective if you are facing **east.** Arrange your candles as stated above and any tools or enhancements that will be in your formation so that they will be in front of you when you are sitting facing east.

Moon Phase

This spell will work best if cast during the **new phase** of the Moon because we are hoping to increase work opportunities just as the Moon is increasing as it waxes to full.

Day of the Week

The most favorable days of the week to cast this spell would be on **Monday, Tuesday, Wednesday, Thursday,** and **Saturday.**

Optional Magickal Enhancements

The following items will add a deeper dimension to your spell and help you to focus yourself more fully, but they are not necessary and the spell can be cast even if you don't have these items available.

Gemstones

The best gemstone to use for this spell is **citrine.**

Incense

Incense that will enhance this spell would be **wisteria.** Place incense in a safe place within your formation if you like; however, start the incense outside of your formation.

Music

If you like music and will not find it distracting, you might want to play something with a **strong beat** like Native American drumming. Whatever you are comfortable with will be best.

Before You Start Your Spell

Make sure you have no distractions.

Turn phones off if possible.

Play soothing music.

Keep the lights dim.

Wash your hands or shower before you begin.

Light incense if you are using it.

Gather everything you need and have it close at hand.

Draw your formation.

Ask your higher power to allow the information to flow through you.

Affirmation

Affirmation to be read within your formation *before you actually begin your spell.*

I recognize to be successful in my own business, I must have a passion and drive for what I am doing. I will take the time to thoroughly study the positives and negatives of my venture.

I understand if I take the chance and follow my bliss, the material gain will follow. When I work with my own passion for something, I am working in sync with the universe.

I know when the universe sends forth a positive desire to act on something, we should not ignore it. It is a direct message, bringing me insight as to whether or not this is my true direction.

If I decide this is my path to happiness, I will proceed and not expect failure. Negative thoughts, anger, fear, and self-pity stop the flow of energy. With positivity I will tune myself to the vibration of success.

AND SO IT IS.

How to Perform the Spell

Once you have cast your formation, light your candles and relax. Write the name of your business on your envelope. If you have not chosen a name, write "my new business" on the envelope. Place your three seeds inside the envelope and seal it.

Now, recite the following incantation:

This business new it starts right here,
Grow and prosper throughout the year,
No stress nor conflict negate my drive
And so it goes, you're now alive.

Conclude with any statement that signifies closure of the ceremony in your mind such as "And so it is," "Blessed be," or "Amen."

Concentrate on what you want your business to accomplish and when you feel you are through, extinguish your candles and release your formation.

After the spell, put the envelope in an area in your home or office where it will not be discarded. A drawer or file cabinet works well. In three months, throw away the envelope and repeat the spell entirely. Only this time include larger seeds (corn kernels, apple seeds, dried whole peas). Do this again three months after that with even larger seeds (pumpkin, sunflower, watermelon), thus completing three spells in one year.

Job Seeking

Necessary Enhancements and Magickal Tools

The necessary tools for this spell include any tools you have chosen for your formation as described below.

- wooden spoon or stick, popsicle stick, coffee stirrer, etc.
- herbs: cinnamon, basil, ginger, cloves (Keep them separate in four separate containers or in four separate envelopes.)
- bowl, glass or wooden, if possible, or any container that you feel is special and can hold the herbs

Candles

You will also need four candles: **green, yellow, orange,** and **white**. Place them on the four sides of the square, not in the corners. You will want the yellow one in front of you facing east, a green candle to the north, orange on the south side, and a white candle behind you to the west.

Formation

All spells should begin with casting a circle, which is your shield of protection. If you are using a triangle or a square, cast your circle first and then cast your formation within it.

The best formation for this spell is the **square.** Cast your formation using methods described in Chapter 5 of the book using a wand, a knife, an extended arm with fingers pointed, salt, or other material items you may have chosen.

Direction to Face

This spell is most effective if you are facing **east.** Arrange your candles as stated above and any tools or enhancements that will be in your formation so that they will be in front of you when you are sitting facing east.

Moon Phase

This spell will work best if cast during the **new** or **waxing phase** of the Moon because we are hoping to increase work opportunities just as the Moon is increasing as it waxes to full.

Day of the Week

The most favorable day of the week to cast this spell would be on **any day but Friday.**

Optional Magickal Enhancements

The following items will add a deeper dimension to your spell and help you to focus yourself more fully, but they are not necessary and the spell can be cast even if you don't have these items available.

Gemstones

The best gemstone to use for this spell is **azurite.** If using additional gemstones other than those recommended in your formation, place them in front of you or in any position your inner self desires.

Incense

Incense that will enhance this spell would be **heliotrope** and **wisteria.** Place incense in a safe place within your formation if you like; however, start the incense outside of your formation.

Music

If you like music and will not find it distracting, you might want to play something instrumental that is **bold** and **rhythmic** with a strong beat. Whatever you are comfortable with will be best.

Before You Start Your Spell

Make sure you have no distractions.

Turn phones off if possible.

Play soothing music.

Keep the lights dim.

Wash your hands or shower before you begin.

Light incense if you are using it.

Gather everything you need and have it close at hand.

Draw your formation.

Ask your higher power to allow the information to flow through you.

Affirmation

Affirmation to be read within your formation *before you actually begin your spell.*

I ask for change. Provide me with clear vision so I do not miss an opportunity that would benefit me. I know success is not solely based on ability. It is determination that is my power. I will listen to my intuition and follow through. If one approach is not working, I will understand the "message" and try a new approach. Bring forth the additional forces I require at this time. Together with the power of the universal life force, I will find the initiative. By the next lunation of the Moon, may I be giving thanks for my new vocation.

AND SO IT IS.

How to Perform the Spell

Once you have cast your formation, relax and center yourself. Light your candles one by one . . . from left to right. Place your herbs one by one into your bowl (order does not matter) and mix them with your wooden spoon or stirrer. Set them to the side.

Now recite the following incantation:

In the present I make a change,
My life for good I now arrange,
Good luck, good fate I know is mine,
Come quickly to me, now's the time.

If you are outside, stand up and throw the herbs into the air in front of you.

If you are inside, extinguish your candles and release your formation. Go outside within the next twenty minutes and throw the mixture into the air. Tossing them out of an open window would also do.

After you throw the mixture, say, "My call is released to the air and so it's done."

Conclude with any statement that signifies closure of the ceremony in your mind such as "And so it is," "Blessed be," or "Amen."

Accepting the Loss of a Job

Necessary Enhancements and Magickal Tools

The necessary tools for this spell include any tools you have chosen for your formation as described below.

You will need:

- something burnable that represents your old job or position: a business card, stationery, or something made of paper (You could even tear a business ad from the Yellow Pages. If you do not have anything, write the name of the company or your position on a piece of paper.)
- fireproof container to burn it in
- matches or a lighter

Candles

You will need three candles: one **black,** one **silver/gray,** and one **white.** Place them in a triangle around you in your formation with the black candle at the left base, the silver/gray at the right base and the white in front of you.

Formation

All spells should begin with casting a circle, which is your shield of protection. If you are using a triangle or a square, cast your circle first and then cast your formation within it.

The best formation for this spell is the **circle.** Cast your formation using methods described in Chapter 5 of the book using a wand, a knife, an extended arm with fingers pointed, salt, or other material items you may have chosen.

Direction to Face

This spell is most effective if you are facing **west.** Arrange your candles as stated above and any tools or enhancements that will be in your formation so that they will be in front of you when you are sitting facing west.

Moon Phase

This spell will work best if cast during the **waning** or **dark phase** of the Moon.

Day of the Week

The most favorable days of the week to cast this spell would be **Tuesday, Wednesday, Thursday,** and **Saturday.**

Optional Magickal Enhancements

The following items will add a deeper dimension to your spell and help you to focus yourself more fully, but they are not necessary and the spell can be cast even if you don't have these items available.

Gemstones

The best gemstone to use for this spell is **silver.** If using additional gemstones other than those recommended in your formation, place them in front of you or in any position your inner self desires.

Incense

Incense that will enhance this spell would be **sage**. Place incense in a safe place within your formation if you like; however, start the incense outside of your formation.

Music

If you like music and will not find it distracting, you might want to play something **classical, New Age,** or any **sounds of nature**. Whatever you are comfortable with will be best.

Before You Start Your Spell

Make sure you have no distractions.

Turn phones off if possible.

Play soothing music.

Keep the lights dim.

Wash your hands or shower before you begin.

Light incense if you are using it.

Gather everything you need and have it close at hand.

Draw your formation.

Ask your higher power to allow the information to flow through you.

Affirmation

Affirmation to be read within your formation *before you actually begin your spell.*

Though my position has been taken from me, I recognize that good has taken place. I will analyze the situation and then let it go. I embrace this opportunity to start again and to grow. I will no longer dwell on the negative aspect; that is now a part of the past. My energy will be applied to thoughts of success in whatever new area I choose. I will not act as a victim and feel sorry for myself. I will not complain to others to find sympathy. I've been given a gift and it will be used to better myself. Nature must have a balance, so if a void is created, it soon will be filled. With joy and enthusiasm, I will heed all openings for potential positions. I give thanks. Surround me with the vibration of success and happiness.

AND SO IT IS.

How to Perform the Spell

Once you have cast your formation, light your candles from left to right and place your gemstones (if using any) in any position your inner self suggests.

Next take the representative of your old job or position and burn it in your fire-burning container.

Then recite the following incantation:

I release this job, it served its time,
A new beginning now is mine.
From ashes will a birth be soon,
I await the next full Moon.

Conclude with any statement that signifies closure of the ceremony in your mind such as "And so it is," "Blessed be," or "Amen."

Now extinguish your candles and release your circle.

Promotion/Raise

Necessary Enhancements and Magickal Tools

The necessary tools for this spell include any tools you have chosen for your formation as described below.

You will need:

- nine dimes

Candles

You will also need a **yellow** candle, a **green** candle, and a **white** candle. Place them in a row in front of you with the yellow to the left, the green in the center, and the white on the right.

Formation

All spells should begin with casting a circle, which is your shield of protection. If you are using a triangle or a square, cast your circle first and then cast your formation within it.

The best formation for this spell is the **square.** Cast your formation using methods described in Chapter 5 of the book using a wand, a knife, an extended arm with fingers pointed, salt, or other material items you may have chosen.

Direction to Face

This spell is most effective if you are facing **east.** Arrange your candles as stated above and any tools or enhancements that will be in your formation so that they will be in front of you when you are sitting facing east.

Moon Phase

This spell will work best if cast during the **waxing phase** of the Moon because we are hoping to increase work opportunities just as the Moon is increasing as it waxes to full.

Day of the Week

The most favorable day of the week to cast this spell would be **on any day but Friday.**

Optional Magickal Enhancements

The following items will add a deeper dimension to your spell and help you to focus yourself more fully, but they are not necessary and the spell can be cast even if you don't have these items available.

Gemstones

The best gemstones to use for this spell are **chrysolite** and **bloodstone.**

Incense

Incense that will enhance this spell would be **spruce.** Place incense in a safe place within your formation if you like; however, start the incense outside of your formation.

Music

If you like music and will not find it distracting, you might want to play something uplifting with **flutes, harps**, and **drums.** Whatever you are comfortable with will be best.

Before You Start Your Spell

Make sure you have no distractions.
Turn phones off if possible.
Play soothing music.
Keep the lights dim.
Wash your hands or shower before you begin.
Light incense if you are using it.
Gather everything you need and have it close at hand.
Draw your formation.
Ask your higher power to allow the information to flow through you.

Affirmation

Affirmation to be read within your formation *before you actually begin your spell.*

Today I put forth to the universe, through the glorious vibration of the Moon, a call for assistance. May my efforts and patience be recognized. I do not come from a place of greed, but I do believe in a fair exchange of energy. I put out more energy in my position than I am receiving back. Balance these scales of fairness within the next nine days. If I meet with something different than I anticipated, I will rethink my situation and approach it from a different angle. I feel the Moon's energy encompassing my needs and acknowledging this request. I am a child of the universe and I know I will be provided for.

AND SO IT IS.

How to Perform the Spell

Light your candles, except for the green one. Set your nine dimes in a circle around your green candle. After they are in place, light the candle.

Then recite the following incantation:

So it is and three times three,
My money increase is to be,
Be not too small, nor too late,
Within nine days I'll know this fate.

Conclude with any statement that signifies closure of the ceremony in your mind such as "And so it is," "Blessed be," or "Amen." Extinguish your candles and release your formation.

Pay attention to the happenings around your work environment in the next nine days.

• 15 •

For Women Only

And you moved among the mysteries,
Absorbed and smiling and sure:
Stirring, tasting, measuring
with the precision of a ritual. . . .

—*Jean Starr Untermeyer*

Women have issues or feelings we often feel only other women can understand. Generally speaking, I feel women express their emotions outwardly more than men. It is also because we ponder our thoughts and feelings more intensely that I feel we can also create positive or negative results more quickly than men. Therefore, as women, we must remember that if you are down on yourself and feel you are a failure in any area of life, this can become a self-fulfilling prophecy and is something to guard against. A ritual can aid you to balance and focus your chaotic energy and open your conscious and subconscious mind to receiving the same message.

Fertility

Necessary Enhancements and Magickal Tools

The necessary tools for this spell include any tools you have chosen for your formation as described below.

You will need:

- poppy, sage, and echinacea—each ingredient in a separate container or separate envelopes
- drawstring bag
- unicorn statue, picture, or some type of representation (represents fertility)

Candles

You will also need three candles: **yellow, red,** and **pink.** Place them in front of you in a row inside your formation with the yellow to the left, the red in the center, and the pink to the right.

Formation

All spells should begin with casting a circle, which is your shield of protection. If you are using a triangle or a square, cast your circle first and then cast your formation within it.

The best formation for this spell is the **circle.** Cast your formation using methods described in Chapter 5 of the book using a wand, a knife, an extended arm with fingers pointed, salt, or other material items you may have chosen.

Direction to Face

This spell is most effective if you are facing **west.** Arrange your candles as stated above and any tools or enhancements that will be in your formation so that they will be in front of you when you are sitting facing west.

Moon Phase

This spell will work best if cast during the **full** or **waxing phase** of the Moon because we are hoping to increase fertility just as the Moon is increasing as it waxes to full.

Day of the Week

The most favorable days of the week to cast this spell would be on **any day but Wednesday.**

Optional Magickal Enhancements

The following items will add a deeper dimension to your spell and help you to focus yourself more fully, but they are not necessary and the spell can be cast even if you don't have these items available.

Gemstones

The best gemstones to use for this spell are **rose quartz** and **turquoise.** If using additional gemstones other than those recommended in your formation, place them in front of you.

Incense

Incense that will enhance this spell would be **hyacinth, myrrh,** and **pine.** Place incense in a safe place within your formation if you like; however, start the incense outside of your formation.

Music

If you like music and will not find it distracting, you might want to play something instrumental that is **peaceful, meditative,** and **calming** with low frequencies. Whatever you are comfortable with will be best.

Before You Start Your Spell

Make sure you have no distractions.
Turn phones off if possible.
Play soothing music.
Keep the lights dim.
Wash your hands or shower before you begin.
Light incense if you are using it.
Gather everything you need and have it close at hand.
Draw your formation.
Ask your higher power to allow the information to flow through you.

Affirmation

Affirmation to be read within your formation *before you actually begin your spell.*

As I sit in the center of this circle, I ask to be blessed with the coming of a child in my life. May my love reach out and encompass this not yet born one.

I see it healthy and happy with the unconditional love around it that I will provide.

May the energy from this circle give me strength and physical well-being so I can carry this child until it makes its entrance into this life.

AND SO IT IS.

How to Perform the Spell

While sitting in your circle, take the three herbs and pour them one by one (in any order) into your drawstring bag. Touch the bag to your stomach for a few seconds, and visualize yourself being pregnant (but do not visualize the gender of the child).

Set the bag down in front of the unicorn and recite the following incantation:

With this radiant Moon a life will grow,
A child is near me that I know.
Happiness, health, and many charms,
I will hold this child in my arms.

Conclude with any statement that signifies closure of the ceremony in your mind such as "And so it is," "Blessed be," or "Amen." Now extinguish your candles and release your formation.

Note: For the next nine days, once a day before bed, lie down and place the bag on your stomach and visualize yourself pregnant. Once you become pregnant, keep the bag until the child is born.

Easy Childbirth

Necessary Enhancements and Magickal Tools

The necessary tools for this spell include any tools you have chosen for your formation as described below.

You will need:

- element water
- a cup to hold it (A large cup is the best for this particular spell as a cup signifies fertility and femininity.)

Candles

You will also need three candles: **blue, pink,** and **orange.** Place them in front of you in a row inside your formation with the blue to the left, the pink in the center, and the orange to the right.

Formation

All spells should begin with casting a circle, which is your shield of protection. If you are using a triangle or a square, cast your circle first and then cast your formation within it.

The best formation for this spell is the **circle.** Cast your formation using methods described in Chapter 5 of the book using a wand, a knife, an extended arm with fingers pointed, salt, or other material items you may have chosen.

Direction to Face

This spell is most effective if you are facing **south.** Arrange your candles as stated above and any tools or enhancements that will be in your formation so that they will be in front of you when you are sitting facing south.

Moon Phase

This spell will work best if cast during the **full, new,** or **waxing phase** of the Moon because we are hoping to increase good possibilities just as the Moon is increasing as it waxes to full.

Day of the Week

Cast this spell on **any day** of the week.

Optional Magickal Enhancements

The following items will add a deeper dimension to your spell and help you to focus yourself more fully, but they are not necessary and the spell can be cast even if you don't have these items available.

Gemstones

The best gemstones to use for this spell are **rose quartz, turquoise,** and **clear quartz crystal.** If using additional gemstones other than those recommended in your formation, place them in front of you.

Incense

Incense that will enhance this spell would be **rose** and **orange.** Place incense in a safe place within your formation if you like; however, start the incense outside of your formation.

Music

If you like music and will not find it distracting, you might want to play something instrumental that is **peaceful, tranquil,** and **calming** with soothing properties like a lullaby that you might find healing. Whatever you are comfortable with will be best.

Before You Start Your Spell

Make sure you have no distractions.

Turn phones off if possible.

Play soothing music.

Keep the lights dim.

Wash your hands or shower before you begin.

Light incense if you are using it.

Gather everything you need and have it close at hand.

Draw your formation.

Ask your higher power to allow the information to flow through you.

Affirmation

Affirmation to be read within your formation *before you actually begin your spell.*

I feel the love of this divine heart. My good thoughts and positive wishes for this unborn child will penetrate my being, and this baby will feel the devotion. The higher power above will protect and guide this new soul into this world with ease and no complications.

AND SO IT IS.

How to Perform the Spell

While within your circle, dip your hands into the element water, touch your bare stomach with the water, and recite the following incantation:

With all the elements of this place,
Your soul arrives through time and space.
You're glad you're here, you're strong and new,
I've said these words and so they're true.

Conclude with any statement that signifies closure of the ceremony in your mind such as "And so it is," "Blessed be," or "Amen." Now extinguish your candles and release your formation.

Throw your element water on a plant or outside. If you must, pour the remaining water down the sink. Gently pass your hand over the drain and say, "back to the earth."

Love (for Women Only)

Necessary Enhancements and Magickal Tools

The necessary tools for this spell include any tools you have chosen for your formation as described below.

You will need:

- dish or arrangement of your favorite flowers, placed in front of you (Real flowers are excellent, but a nice, clean artificial arrangement also works nicely.)

Candles

You will also need one **pink** candle placed in front of you.

Formation

All spells should begin with casting a circle, which is your shield of protection. If you are using a triangle or a square, cast your circle first and then cast your formation within it.

The best formation for this spell is the **circle.** Cast your formation using methods described in Chapter 5 of the book using a wand, a knife, an extended arm with fingers pointed, salt, or other material items you may have chosen.

Direction to Face

This spell is most effective if you are facing **south.** Arrange your candles as stated above and any tools or enhancements that will be in your formation so that they will be in front of you when you are sitting facing south.

Moon Phase

This spell will work best if cast during the **full, new,** or **waxing phase** of the Moon because we are hoping to increase good possibilities just as the Moon is increasing as it waxes to full.

Day of the Week

The most favorable days of the week to cast this spell would be on **Sunday, Tuesday Friday,** or **Saturday.**

Optional Magickal Enhancements

The following items will add a deeper dimension to your spell and help you to focus yourself more fully, but they are not necessary and the spell can be cast even if you don't have these items available.

Gemstones

The best gemstones to use for this spell are **rose quartz, carnelian,** and **clear quartz crystal.** If using additional gemstones other than those recommended in your formation, place them in front of you.

Incense

Incense that will enhance this spell would be **musk, myrrh, rose,** and **pine.** Place incense in a safe place within your formation if you like; however, start the incense outside of your formation.

Music

If you like music and will not find it distracting, you might want to play something instrumental that is **slow, meditative,** and **peaceful.** Whatever you are comfortable with will be best.

Before You Start Your Spell

Make sure you have no distractions.
Turn phones off if possible.
Play soothing music.
Keep the lights dim.
Wash your hands or shower before you begin.
Light incense if you are using it.
Gather everything you need and have it close at hand.
Draw your formation.
Ask your higher power to allow the information to flow through you.

Affirmation

Affirmation to be read within your formation *before you actually begin your spell.*

I am infused with energy when I think of the love in my life that I not only receive but I also give to others. I welcome the vibration of additional love into my existence, and I look forward to sending more love out to others.

Whether I am alone or have an entire support system of people, I am still always loved and capable of loving. I love the flowers and the trees and all of nature. I love my higher power that loves me unconditionally.

I love my feminine intuition that serves me well, when I listen to it. People who have made the transition to the other side love me. They still guide and help me.

Love is my antidote for all that weakens me.

AND SO IT IS.

How to Perform the Spell

Recite the following incantation:

Like a healing stream may love keep flowing,
With love comes wisdom and a knowing
That each day and every hour,
I draw the energy of feminine power.

Conclude with any statement that signifies closure of the ceremony in your mind such as "And so it is," "Blessed be," or "Amen." Now extinguish your candles and release your formation.

16

For Men Only

To become a thoroughly good man is the best prescription for keeping a sound mind in a sound body.

—Bowen

There are many support groups and sympathetic attitudes for women but fewer such groups for men. As a woman, I must admit men cannot be all things to everybody and be strong and emotionless like some deem they should. Men sometimes do not even have the choices women do. A woman has the legal right to decide whether she is going to be a mother or not. However, the man does not have that same choice. If the woman decides she wants a child, he is a father, technically, whether he wants to be or not.

This is a controversial subject; and I just recently read an interesting point of view that some say there is no difference between a women terminating pregnancy and a man walking away from fathering a child that he simply does not want.

That being said, the spells below are for the men who want to be fathers and feel that fathering is important to them, whether they are there full-time or just on occasion. However, I am not judging, as I see both points of view.

The love spell is something for all men to consider as it is truly an emotional awakening and brings blessings and harmony.

Fathering

Necessary Enhancements and Magickal Tools

The necessary tools for this spell include any tools you have chosen for your formation as described below.

Candles

You will need one **pink** candle placed in front of you.

Formation

All spells should begin with casting a circle, which is your shield of protection. If you are using a triangle or a square, cast your circle first and then cast your formation within it.

The best formation for this spell is the **circle.** Cast your formation using methods described in Chapter 5 of the book using a wand, a knife, an extended arm with fingers pointed, salt, or other material items you may have chosen.

Direction to Face

This spell is most effective if you are facing **south.** Arrange your candles as stated above and any tools or enhancements that will be in your formation so that they will be in front of you when you are sitting facing south.

Moon Phase

This spell will work best if cast during the **full, new,** or **waxing phase** of the Moon because we are hoping to increase good possibilities just as the Moon is increasing as it waxes to full.

Day of the Week

The most favorable days of the week to cast this spell would be on **Sunday, Tuesday, Friday,** or **Saturday.**

Optional Magickal Enhancements

The following items will add a deeper dimension to your spell and help you to focus yourself more fully, but they are not necessary and the spell can be cast even if you don't have these items available.

Gemstones

The best gemstones to use for this spell are **rose quartz** and

carnelian. If using additional gemstones other than those recommended in your formation, place them in front of you.

Incense

Incense that will enhance this spell would be **rosemary** and **lilac.** Place incense in a safe place within your formation if you like; however, start the incense outside of your formation.

Music

If you like music and will not find it distracting, you might want to play something instrumental with **bamboo flutes** or **panpipes.** Whatever you are comfortable with will be best.

Before You Start Your Spell

Make sure you have no distractions.
Turn phones off if possible.
Play soothing music.
Keep the lights dim.
Wash your hands or shower before you begin.
Light incense if you are using it.
Gather everything you need and have it close at hand.
Draw your formation.
Ask your higher power to allow the information to flow through you.

Affirmation

Affirmation to be read within your formation *before you actually begin your spell.*

As a father, remind me to give my time and attention to my child/children so there will never be the feeling of abandonment. Although sometimes a challenge, our children are a product of their experiences; and may the experiences my child/children have with me be those of love and sympathy. It is important for me to support their free expression as this will promote self-worth. I will love my child/children for who they are and not what I think they should be and will acknowledge the smallest of accomplishments. I give more to my children when I give them my time and support—there is no substitute.

AND SO IT IS.

How to Perform the Spell

Recite the following incantation:

A father, I am, such as it be.
Understanding and love emerge from me.
May the universe to my children reveal,
The love I possess, the way that I feel.

Close your eyes and visualize your children or child healthy, happy, and smiling.

Conclude with any statement that signifies closure of the ceremony in your mind such as "And so it is," "Blessed be," or "Amen." Now extinguish your candles and release your formation.

Love (for Men Only)

Necessary Enhancements and Magickal Tools

The necessary tools for this spell include any tools you have chosen for your formation as described below.

Candles

You will need one **pink** candle placed in front of you.

Formation

All spells should begin with casting a circle, which is your shield of protection. If you are using a triangle or a square, cast your circle first and then cast your formation within it.

The best formation for this spell is the **circle.** Cast your formation using methods described in Chapter 5 of the book using a wand, a knife, an extended arm with fingers pointed, salt, or other material items you may have chosen.

Direction to Face

This spell is most effective if you are facing **south.** Arrange your candles as stated above and any tools or enhancements that will be in your formation so that they will be in front of you when you are sitting facing south.

Moon Phase

This spell will work best if cast during the **full, new,** or **waxing phase** of the Moon because we are hoping to increase good possibilities just as the Moon is increasing as it waxes to full.

Day of the Week

The most favorable days of the week to cast this spell would be on **Sunday, Tuesday, Friday,** or **Saturday.**

Optional Magickal Enhancements

The following items will add a deeper dimension to your spell and help you to focus yourself more fully, but they are not necessary and the spell can be cast even if you don't have these items available.

Gemstones

The best gemstones to use for this spell are **rose quartz, carnelian,** and **clear quartz crystal.** If using additional gemstones other than those recommended in your formation, place them in front of you.

Incense

Incense that will enhance this spell would be **rosemary** and **lilac.** Place incense in a safe place within your formation if you like; however, start the incense outside of your formation.

Music

If you like music and will not find it distracting, you might want to play something instrumental that is romantic with a **panpipe** or **bamboo flute.**

Before You Start Your Spell

Make sure you have no distractions.

Turn phones off if possible.

Play soothing music.

Keep the lights dim.

Wash your hands or shower before you begin.

Light incense if you are using it.

Gather everything you need and have it close at hand.

Draw your formation.

Ask your higher power to allow the information to flow through you.

Affirmation

Affirmation to be read within your formation *before you actually begin your spell.*

The more loving I am to others, the more it will come back to me. However, I do not give love for the reason of receiving but simply for the joy of lending of my time and myself.

I open myself to accepting the positives and negatives of people. When I worry about the people who love me or who I love, it serves no purpose and leaves me helpless.

Therefore, I choose to send them loving thoughts and powerful blessings that I know they will receive instantaneously.

When I am sad or mournful, I am not ashamed of crying as I know this is release that all humans should utilize. If I were not capable of love, I would not have these emotions. It is love that keeps me walking on the path to higher purpose. My way may not be the way of someone else; but if I walk in love and light, I will be love and light to others.

How to Perform the Spell

Recite the following incantation:

This Moon above gives me the light,
To see the love during day or night.
I hold it close, I know it dear,
Love protects, I have no fear.

Conclude with any statement that signifies closure of the ceremony in your mind such as "And so it is," "Blessed be," or "Amen." Now extinguish your candles and release your formation.

17

Spirituality

Our Thought is the key which unlocks the doors of the world. There is something in us which corresponds to that which is around us, beneath us, and above us.

—Samuel McCord Crothers

Spiritual spells are personally my favorite, as they are always so mysterious and enlightening. "When we pray, we ask; when we meditate, we listen." But when we spin a spell or ritual, we ask . . . we listen . . . and we do. It's a trinity of information and execution. If you were to pick only one spell in this entire book to perform, I would recommend the spell on "divine messages"; it is here that all may become clear.

Seeking Your Purpose

Necessary Enhancements and Magickal Tools

The necessary tools for this spell include any tools you have chosen for your formation as described below.

You must have:

- a small clear quartz crystal and a small piece of amethyst
- a drawstring bag or something that holds them together (A handkerchief or piece of cloth would work; however, do not put them in the bag yet.)

Candles

You will also need one **purple** candle placed in front of you.

Formation

All spells should begin with casting a circle, which is your shield of protection. If you are using a triangle or a square, cast your circle first and then cast your formation within it.

The best formation for this spell is the **triangle** or a **circle.** Cast your formation using methods described in Chapter 5 of the book using a wand, a knife, an extended arm with fingers pointed, salt, or other material items you may have chosen.

Direction to Face

This spell is most effective if you are facing **east.** Arrange your candles as stated above and any tools or enhancements that will be in your formation so that they will be in front of you when you are sitting facing east.

Moon Phase

This spell will work best if cast during the **full** or **waxing phase** of the Moon because we are hoping to increase good possibilities just as the Moon is increasing as it waxes to full.

Day of the Week

The most favorable days of the week to cast this spell would be on **Sunday, Monday,** or **Thursday.**

Optional Magickal Enhancements

The following items will add a deeper dimension to your spell and help you to focus yourself more fully, but they are not necessary and the spell can be cast even if you don't have these items available.

Gemstones

The best gemstone to use for this spell is **amethyst** or **clear quartz crystal.** If using additional gemstones other than those recommended in your formation, place them in front of you.

Incense

Incense that will enhance this spell would be **frankincense, sweetgrass,** or **sage.** Place incense in a safe place within your formation if you like; however, start the incense outside of your formation.

Music

If you like music and will not find it distracting, you might want to play something instrumental that is **meditative** and **peaceful**, perhaps sounds of the ocean. Whatever you are comfortable with will be best.

Before You Start Your Spell

Make sure you have no distractions.
Turn phones off if possible.
Play soothing music.
Keep the lights dim.
Wash your hands or shower before you begin.
Light incense if you are using it.
Gather everything you need and have it close at hand.
Draw your formation.
Ask your higher power to allow the information to flow through you.

Affirmation

Affirmation to be read within your formation *before you actually begin your spell.*

In the luminous rays of the Moon, I ask with somewhat a sense of frustration: Why am I here? What is my purpose? Do I have a special place or goal I should be pursuing?

Am I being anxious, for I have not yet found this special accomplishment I am to bring into being? Am I pressing something that is not yet to be revealed to me? Do I feel, as the years march on, that the time is now because I say it is now? I don't know. Tell me, help me, and bring me clarity.

Perhaps I am already doing what I am meant to do. Perhaps my vanity thinks I should be contributing on a much higher level. Everyone has his or her purpose. I look at nature. The ants have their place and so do the eagles.

Will I change the world? Am I meant to be a support person for someone else? Am I helping the planet every time I give a warm smile and nod to a stranger? Must everything be so grand, as for all people to see our good deeds and acknowledge them? Maybe I already am fulfilling my purpose and am not aware of it. Bring me guidance through the wisdom of the all-knowing beings and energies that are enlightened. Make me aware if I have already reached my goal or if I am about to enter onto the path that leads toward it.

My age and desire have nothing to do with it. It is my higher power that knows the way.

I will be patient. In my patience I will learn what my true purpose is. I let go of the desire to know and accept that things will evolve according to the universal plan. I am here, I am ready.

AND SO IT IS.

How to Perform the Spell

Take your gemstones and place them in your bag or cloth. While holding the bag, recite the following incantation:

These stones I hold are conductors too,
With answers and visions that will come through.
In my dreams, I will see what's real,
My destiny to be revealed.

Conclude with any statement that signifies closure of the ceremony in your mind such as "And so it is," "Blessed be," or "Amen." Now extinguish your candles and release your formation.

Sleep with the bag of stones under your pillow or next to the bed.

Pay attention to your dreams for the next three days. Look for the symbols within your dreams. The answers are there for you.

Divine Messages

Necessary Enhancements and Magickal Tools

The necessary tools for this spell include any tools you have chosen for your formation as described below.

You will need:

- tarot cards
- scrying mirror (black mirror that reflects), crystal, or anything you can see into

(If you do not have any of these forms of divination, take a bowl and fill it halfway with water. You will use the reflection of the water to pick up images.)

Candles

You will also need one **purple** candle placed in front of you and to the left and one **yellow** candle placed in front of you and to the right.

Formation

All spells should begin with casting a circle, which is your shield of protection. If you are using a triangle or a square, cast your circle first and then cast your formation within it.

The best formation for this spell is the **triangle** or a **circle.** Cast your formation using methods described in Chapter 5 of the book using a wand, a knife, an extended arm with fingers pointed, salt, or other material items you may have chosen.

Direction to Face

This spell is most effective if you are facing **south.** Arrange your candles as stated above and any tools or enhancements that will be in your formation so that they will be in front of you when you are sitting facing south.

Moon Phase

This spell will work best if cast during the **full** or **waxing phase** of the Moon because we are hoping to increase good possibilities just as the Moon is increasing as it waxes to full.

Day of the Week

The most favorable days of the week to cast this spell would be on **Sunday, Monday, Thursday,** or **Friday.**

Optional Magickal Enhancements

The following items will add a deeper dimension to your spell and help you to focus yourself more fully, but they are not necessary and the spell can be cast even if you don't have these items available.

Gemstones

The best gemstone to use for this spell is **green tourmaline** or **beryl.** If using additional gemstones other than those recommended in your formation, place them in front of you.

Incense

Incense that will enhance this spell would be **wisteria.** Place incense in a safe place within your formation if you like; however, start the incense outside of your formation.

Music

If you like music and will not find it distracting, you might want to play something instrumental that is meditative and soothing like **harp** or **flute.** Whatever you are comfortable with will be best.

Before You Start Your Spell

Make sure you have no distractions.
Turn phones off if possible.
Play soothing music.
Keep the lights dim.
Wash your hands or shower before you begin.
Light incense if you are using it.
Gather everything you need and have it close at hand.
Draw your formation.
Ask your higher power to allow the information to flow through you.

Affirmation

Affirmation to be read within your formation *before you actually begin your spell.*

I am seated here in peace and contentment. I am prepared to receive all messages being sent to me. I embrace the message I will receive tonight. I am not seeking anything in particular. I am tuned into what my higher power chooses to share. I will not attempt to guess what it will be. Bring it forth strong, loud, and clear. I will hear for I am in tune with the way of the universal life force energy. Let it flow. I am listening, I understand, I want to see the light, the way, and the balance. I will now sit in silence and concentrate.

I beckon the message to come forth.

How to Perform the Spell

Now recite the following incantation:

Through this channel bring a view,
Be it bright, and be it true.
With visions dancing on this night,
My message here is now in sight.

If you are using tarot cards or regular playing cards, pull only three and pick up the messages in the way you were taught to read them. If using a scrying mirror, crystal, or a bowl of water, stare down into it. Try to throw your eyes almost out of focus and see if you can pick up any images. (This takes a bit of practice unless you have been doing it for quite some time, so if you do not see anything the first time, repeat the spell on a different day and try again.) If none of these methods of "seeing" work for you, say, "Send my messages to my dreams, the next full Moon." Note on the calendar when the next full Moon is and see what your dreams tell you.

Conclude with any statement that signifies closure of the ceremony in your mind such as "And so it is," "Blessed be," or "Amen." Now extinguish your candles and release your formation.

Group Meditation/Spell for Any Purpose

Necessary Tools and Enhancements

None are necessary unless the group decides on something.

Day of the Week

This spell should be performed on any day the full Moon is present.

Formation

All spells should begin with casting a circle, which is your shield of protection. If you are using a triangle or a square, cast your circle first and then cast your formation within it.

The best formation for this spell is the **circle.** Cast your formation using methods described in Chapter 5 of the book using a wand, a knife, an extended arm with fingers pointed, salt, or other material items you may have chosen.

Moon Phase

This spell will work best if cast during the **full phase** of the Moon.

Direction to Face

Any direction is fine.

How to Conduct a Group Meditation/Spell

A group meditation consists of two or more people.

When working with a group, it's best to have everyone clear their schedule of other commitments that night: This is why it is important to plan ahead. Nevertheless, in our busy lives, it is understandable that we may have family obligations, jobs, and other commitments. Hence, we may not have the luxury of dedicating the entire evening to this spell. If this is the case, allow at least three hours from start to finish and remember to adjust for travel time if necessary.

Decide why you are gathering, such as world peace or the recovery of a special person, etc. One individual must be appointed as the group leader or facilitator. This person is responsible for everything being in place and in order. This should be worked out well in advance of the session.

Also, the group leader or someone else must create the meditation/spell or incantation and write it down on paper for the leader to read. It may be as simple as: "We gather here tonight to generate the vibration of world peace to the entire planet. And so it is." Or it can be much more elaborate.

Whether you will stand, sit, or hold hands is up to the group or the organizer. In this particular meditation/spell, sometimes sitting is considered the best because you will be in an altered state and could lose your balance. Whatever the decision, make the choice in advance. Once everyone is in place, the facilitator should take his or her spot in the configuration and begin the meditation/spell, speaking the following in a calm, slow voice. This person should not stand in the center with his or her back to anyone. He or she should be part of the circle.

How to Perform the Spell

The facilitator casts the circle in the normal way. The group leader says:

"Close your eyes. As I count up from one to ten, imagine yourself leaving your physical body and drawing closer to the Moon.

"One—Breathe deeply—exhale slowly.

"Two—Breathe deeply—exhale again slowly.

"Three—Feel yourself ascending toward the light of the Moon.

"Four—Sense the energy of the Moon coming nearer and nearer.

"Five—Continue to keep your eyes closed, and exhale slowly.

"Six—As you exhale, imagine any negativity that you now carry or have held on to from the past leaving you.

"Seven—Feel the vibration of the Moon's light. The earth is below. You are very safe—a white light encompasses you.

"Eight—You are now connected with the Moon's positive energy. Envision yourself on this luminous sphere. Are you sitting, standing, walking, or merely next to it? Imagine where you are.

"Nine—Keep your eyes closed. Absorb the power, the life force. You are now part of that life force energy, not just an onlooker. You are one with the universe. Take a moment and just be. Try not to think or imagine anything.

(Facilitator should allow for about five to ten seconds of silence.)

"Ten—Continue to keep your eyes closed, and I will now recite our meditation. Concentrate."

(The facilitator recites the spell/meditation at this point. At the end of the meditation, the facilitator says, "And so it is." The group may repeat those words.)

The facilitator now recites:

"We must now slowly return from this level of mind. As I count back from ten to one, see yourself descending to the earth.

"Ten, nine, eight, seven—the Moon's energy is still with you . . . Six, five, four—visualize our group below. Three, two—you are now back in your body. One—open your eyes."

At this point, the facilitator can allow people to do what they wish. Some will stay in their position and gaze at the Moon. Some groups enjoy staying in the configuration and discussing what they have just experienced. In this case, talking should be encouraged. All should agree in advance as to what will be suitable.

Remember to release your formation, extinguish all candles, and leave the area clean. Always have respect for yourself, others, and the planet.

18

Miscellaneous Spells

Your heart's desire be with you!

—Shakespeare

This chapter includes spells that don't quite fit into any special category in the setup of this book, but they are some of the most powerful spells and should be examined closely. Other than the "binding spell," which is only for extenuating circumstances, every spell in this section has been well received and the testimonies and feedback have always been tremendous. If you have no special needs from the other categories but enjoy casting spells, utilize these and feel what it is like to be a magickal trailblazer!

Better Communication

Necessary Enhancements and Magickal Tools

The necessary tools for this spell include any tools you have chosen for your formation as described below.

You will need:

- a pen
- a bowl
- whole bay leaves (You can buy them in any grocery store in the spice section in jars. You should have extra on hand in your formation. You may also wish to have something to grind up the leaves when you finish the spell, like a mortar and pestle or a chili grinder—it will depend on how crumbly your leaves are.)

Candles

You will also need four candles set on the four sides of the square.

A **blue** candle on the east side, **brown** to the north, **silver /gray** on the west side, and **white** on the south side in front of you.

Formation

All spells should begin with casting a circle, which is your shield of protection. If you are using a triangle or a square, cast your circle first and then cast your formation within it.

The best formation for this spell is the **square.** Cast your formation using methods described in Chapter 5 of the book using a wand, a knife, an extended arm with fingers pointed, salt, or other material items you may have chosen.

Direction to Face

This spell is most effective if you are facing **south.** Arrange your candles as stated above and any tools or enhancements that will be in your formation so that they will be in front of you when you are sitting facing south.

Moon Phase

This spell will work best if cast during the **waxing phase** of the Moon because you are trying to increase something as the Moon increases to fullness.

Day of the Week

Cast this spell on **any day** of the week.

Optional Magickal Enhancements

The following items will add a deeper dimension to your spell and help you to focus yourself more fully, but they are not necessary and the spell can be cast even if you don't have these items available.

Gemstones

The best gemstones to use for this spell are **sapphire, green tourmaline,** and **beryl.** If using additional gemstones other than those recommended in your formation, place them in front of you.

Incense

Incense that will enhance this spell would be **wisteria.** Place incense in a safe place within your formation if you like; however, start the incense outside of your formation.

Music

If you like music and will not find it distracting, you might want to play something **classical, acoustic,** or **New Age.** Whatever you are comfortable with will be best.

Before You Start Your Spell

Make sure you have no distractions.
Turn phones off if possible.
Play soothing music.
Keep the lights dim.
Wash your hands or shower before you begin.
Light incense if you are using it.
Gather everything you need and have it close at hand.
Draw your formation.
Ask your higher power to allow the information to flow through you.

Affirmation

Affirmation to be read within your formation *before you actually begin your spell.*

Within this place where I am today, I now look for answers. I feel the wisdom of my guides and my higher power. I feel the source from which all life comes. I am struggling with an issue that better communication may help to resolve. Send me thoughts, send me words, send me strength to do what is best for everyone concerned.

I will make all efforts to tell (person's name) about my concern, which is (state concern).

I will have the presence of mind to confront him/her when the mood is calm and no distractions engulf us. I will express my feelings calmly without using words that sound judgmental or critical. I will not be hurtful or put guilt on (person's name). I want to improve the situation, not fill it with more pain. With this Moon's reflection here today, help me say what is needed to be said. If (person's name) chooses not to answer or work with me, I must then make a choice. I will have done everything I can to resolve this situation. But now it requires both of us to work together to triumph.

I feel true insight surrounding me. I greet you. Show me new pathways; bring me clarity. Help me overcome any weakness to speak my mind. I will take the initiative to start communicating. If it does not bring resolution, then perhaps it's not meant to be.

Send forth the answers by the next cycle of the Moon. Fill me with new ideas and guidance.

AND SO IT IS.

How to Perform the Spell

Take your bay leaf and write the person's first name on the leaf the best you can. If the leaf falls apart, start again with a new leaf and just use the first initial. You must write gently!

Crush the bay leaf into the bowl with your hands or any other kitchen tool that you have available that you would use to smash or crush herbs.

Then recite the following incantation:

May the winds and air send my plea,
Feel my thought coming to thee.
Travel with the speed of light,
Hear it, sense it, here tonight.

Take your crushed bay leaf and blow it out of your hand into the air if you are outside.

If you are inside, after your spell is through, go outside for a moment or open a door or window and do the same.

Conclude with any statement that signifies closure of the ceremony in your mind such as, "And so it is," "Blessed be," or "Amen." Now extinguish your candles and release your formation.

Birthday Spell

The day of your birth is certainly a time to acknowledge your own power and cast a spell for well-being throughout the coming year. This spell may be conducted on the actual day of your birthday or the month in which you were born.

As you are aware of your desires and aspirations better than anyone else, in this birthday spell, you write your own personal request.

Necessary Enhancements and Magickal Tools

The necessary tools for this spell include any tools you have chosen for your formation as described below.

- fire-burning container and matches
- a very small piece of some sweet food you enjoy (You might choose cake, pie, pastry, or a piece of soft candy. If you cannot eat sweets, use a piece of cheese or something small you enjoy.)

- water
- wine or fruit juice (color doesn't matter)
- three pieces of paper and pen or pencil
- a brick, stone, or piece of wood (the size is not important)

Candles

You will need three candles; **red, white,** and **yellow.** Set them in a triangle in front of you with the red to the lower left, white in the middle (at the point of the triangle facing north), and yellow to the lower right.

Formation

All spells should begin with casting a circle, which is your shield of protection. If you are using a triangle or a square, cast your circle first and then cast your formation within it.

The best formation for this spell is the **circle.** Cast your formation using methods described in Chapter 5 of the book using a wand, a knife, an extended arm with fingers pointed, salt, or other material items you may have chosen.

Direction to Face

This spell is most effective if you are facing **north.** Arrange your candles and any tools or enhancements that will be in your formation as stated above so that they will be in front of you when you are sitting facing north.

Moon Phase

This spell can be done **anytime** (after all, it is your birthday!).

Day of the Week

Cast this spell on **any day** of the week.

Optional Magickal Enhancements

The following items will add a deeper dimension to your spell and help you to focus yourself more fully, but they are not necessary and the spell can be cast even if you don't have these items available.

Gemstones

The best gemstone to use for this spell is your **birthstone.** The following list gives the meaning of each stone, as well as birth flowers, which can also be used for the spell.

Birthstones and Birth Flowers

Month	Stone	Flower
January	Garnet (Constancy)	Carnation
February	Amethyst (Sincerity)	Violet
March	Bloodstone (Courage)	Jonquil
April	Diamond (Innocence)	Sweet Pea
May	Emerald (Success in Love)	Lily of the Valley
June	Pearl (Health)	Rose
July	Ruby (Contented Mind)	Larkspur
August	Sardonyx (Conjugal Felicity)	Gladiola
September	Sapphire (Love)	Aster
October	Opal (Hope)	Calendula
November	Topaz (Fidelity)	Chrysanthemum
December	Turquoise (Prosperity)	Narcissus

There are different schools of thought and birthstones may differ depending on the source you consult, but I think this is a fairly common assortment. Feel free to research this further if you like.

Incense

Incense that will enhance this spell would be any **citrus.** Place incense in a safe place within your formation if you like; however, start the incense outside of your formation.

Music

If you like music and will not find it distracting, you might want to play something instrumental that is **happy** and **peaceful.** Whatever you are comfortable with will be best.

Before You Start Your Birthday Spell

Make sure you have no distractions.
Turn phones off if possible.
Play soothing music.
Keep the lights dim.
Wash your hands or shower before you begin.
Light incense if you are using it.
Gather everything you need and have it close at hand.
Draw your formation.
Ask your higher power to allow the information to flow through you.

How to Perform the Spell

Write down three goals, hopes, or desires on three separate pieces of paper. (If you prefer, you may type them out in advance.) We utilize the vibration of the number three as this is a number of abundance and multiplication.

Take the papers with your hopes in hand, and one by one recite them out loud or to yourself. After reading each desire, burn it in your fire-burning container.

When you have burned all three papers, recite the following incantation:

I send out my wishes . . . desires three,
May they disperse and come back to me.

Next:

Say, "May I never be hungry." Eat a bit of your cake.

Say, "May I never be thirsty." Take a sip of your water.

Say, "May I never be homeless." Tap your brick, wood, or stone three times with your hand.

Light your red candle and say, "May I always be blessed with physical health."

Light your yellow candle and say, "May I always be blessed with emotional health."

Light your white candle and say, "May I always be blessed with spiritual health."

Take a sip of your wine or fruit juice and say:

I celebrate myself today,
I am renewed today,
I follow a divinely directed path today.

Conclude with any statement that signifies closure of the ceremony in your mind such as, "And so it is," "Blessed be," or "Amen." Extinguish your candles and release your formation.

Dispose of the ashes any way you see fit—the message has already been sent through the smoke while they were burning.

Freeing Yourself from Someone (A Binding Spell)

Warning to the reader: This spell is irreversible and should be not be treated lightly. It is not a spell for anyone who is not a mature adult with some wisdom and understanding of life as a part of their experience. Binding spells are very controversial. I truly gave the notion of putting a binding spell in this book a lot of thought. However, through meditation and divine advice, I decided to include it.

The intention of this spell is to stop a person that is trying to harm you mentally, physically, spiritually, or is perhaps having thoughts of harming themselves. However, the well-justified controversy lies in the fact that you may be wrong about that person. If you are not sure whether to perform a binding spell or not . . . do not. Instead, conduct the White Light Protection Spell found in this chapter. It may be more suitable.

Understand totally and without doubt that this is by *no means* an alternative to seeking help from law enforcement professionals, counselors, or advisors. Do not think of this as protection, or you will have a false sense of security! The intention here is to add extra strength and energy to the commonsense precautions you already have in effect. Only perform this spell after you have done everything possible within the means of the law and society to keep this person away from you. This spell is *not* meant to keep away pesky callers, visitors, or anyone you simply get agitated with or even downright angry with . . . it is much too powerful.

Necessary Enhancements and Magickal Tools

The necessary tools for this spell include any tools you have chosen for your formation as described below.

You will need:

- effigy or poppet* (see illustration above)
- cord, string, yarn, or something you can tie the poppet with
- salt

*In this case, you should make a doll with two arms, two legs, and a head. You can hand sew something and stuff it for bulk, or you can cut one out of cardboard or something strong. Write the person's name on the poppet or place their picture on it in some fashion. A poppet can also be made of corn husks or any other material that can look like a human form.

The idea of a poppet or doll effigy may make some people nervous since they associate this practice with voodoo. This is not voodoo, but the fact that this spell uses a doll figure and these are also used in voodoo makes this concern understandable. However, you are using it to protect yourself and are not inflicting harm on anyone. You are binding them from harming you or themselves.

(At this point, if the idea of this binding spell is not comfortable, do not do it.)

Candles

You will also need one **black** candle placed in front of you.

Formation

All spells should begin with casting a circle, which is your shield of protection. If you are using a triangle or a square, cast your circle first and then cast your formation within it.

The best formation for this spell is the **triangle.** Cast your formation using methods described in Chapter 5 of the book using a wand, a knife, an extended arm with fingers pointed, salt, or other material items you may have chosen.

Direction to Face

This spell is most effective if you are facing **west.** Arrange your candles as stated above and any tools or enhancements that will be in your formation so that they will be in front of you when you are sitting facing west.

Moon Phase

This spell will work best if cast during the **waning** or **dark phase** of the Moon.

Day of the Week

The most favorable days of the week to cast this spell would be on **Sunday** or **Saturday.**

Optional Magickal Enhancements

The following items will add a deeper dimension to your spell and help you to focus yourself more fully, but they are not necessary. The spell can be cast even if you don't have these items available.

Gemstones

The best gemstones to use for this spell are **jet, obsidian,** and **clear quartz crystal.** If using additional gemstones other than those recommended in your formation, place them in front of you.

Incense

Incense that will enhance this spell would be **rosewood** and **lavender.** Place incense in a safe place within your formation if you like; however, start the incense outside of your formation.

Music

If you like music and will not find it distracting, you might want to play something instrumental that is low frequency, **peaceful,** and **soothing.** Whatever you are comfortable with will be best.

Before You Start Your Spell

Make sure you have no distractions.
Turn phones off if possible.
Play soothing music.
Keep the lights dim.
Wash your hands or shower before you begin.
Light incense if you are using it.
Gather everything you need and have it close at hand.
Draw your formation.
Ask your higher power to allow the information to flow through you.

Affirmation

Affirmation to be read within your formation *before you actually begin your spell.*

The reason I have chosen to cast this special spell is because I feel I have no alternative and have examined all possibilities. Before I continue this ritual that cannot be reversed, I will reflect to see if this is the correct choice. If I change my mind, I will instead use a spell of protection. It is now I will decide if I want to perform this powerful action.

(If you decide not to, it may be for the best.)

How to Perform the Spell

1. Light your black candle now.
2. Take your poppet and wrap your cord, string, or ribbon around it. While you wrap the cord around, say, "I bind you (person's name) from hurting yourself or others." You must bind the arms and legs together and cover the entire head area with the string, meaning anything that could harm someone must not be left dangling free.
3. Sprinkle salt on the poppet.
4. Now say again: "I bind you, (person's name), from hurting others or yourself."

Now recite the following incantation:

As this cord is wound,
So are you bound.
From me you're sealed,
My strength revealed.
Harm you none and stay away,
You're powerless as of today.

Conclude with any statement that signifies closure of the ceremony in your mind such as, "And so it is," "Blessed be," or "Amen." Now extinguish your candles and release your formation.

Take the poppet and bury it off the property where you live or if you have a fireplace or large outside burner, you can opt to burn it. Remember you are not harming anyone, only stopping future actions.

Increasing Your Psychic Abilities/Invoking the Power Within

This spell will help give you confidence to further pursue and expand your psychic abilities. It will also increase your inclination to experiment with new forms of divination. It will aid in opening your third eye, which is your intuitive eye and the center of your psychic power, where information beyond the psychical world comes from. The Third Eye is located in the middle of your forehead between the eyebrows. It is etheric and obviously not visible. The Third Eye is also considered your sixth chakra, which is a type of spinning energy vortex that is invisible within the body.

If you are drawn to becoming more intuitive, perform this spell and invoke the power. Your talent is the call.

Do not rush this spell. Take your time and do this *alone* or with *a person of the opposite sex,* thereby using the energy of the masculine and the feminine, the yin and the yang vital force.

Necessary Enhancements and Magickal Tools

The necessary tools for this spell include any tools you have chosen for your formation as described below.

All of the tools should be set in front of the person on a floor, table, or altar.

You will need:

- wine or fruit juice (white or red)
- special glass or chalice for the wine or juice (If you perform this spell with someone else, you may choose to drink from the same chalice, mixing your energies.)
- incense, cologne, perfume, or something you can smell is a must in this ritual (If you do not like the aroma of the suggested incense, use anything you find pleasant.)
- deep purple colored cloth (silk, velvet, felt, or something soft), any size
- bell, gong, or chime (Sometimes wind chimes will work if you do not have an individual bell. Note: If you are using large wind chimes, you may have to lay them on the ground if there is nowhere to hang them within your circle. You just need to make sure you can strike them together or hit them with something so they make a ringing tone. A good suggestion is to cast your formation right below them so you merely have to stand up to tap them.)

You may want to include tools of divination to be used after the spell, such as cards, runes, crystals, and so on.

Candles

You will also need three candles: **purple, orange,** and **white.** Set them in a row in front of you with the purple to the left, the white in the middle, and the orange to the right.

Formation

All spells should begin with casting a circle, which is your shield of protection. If you are using a triangle or a square, cast your circle first and then cast your formation within it.

The best formation for this spell is the **triangle.** Cast your formation using methods described in Chapter 5 of the book using a wand, a knife, an extended arm with fingers pointed, salt, or other material items you may have chosen.

Direction to Face

This spell is most effective if you are facing **north.** Arrange your candles as stated above and any tools or enhancements that will be in your formation so that they will be in front of you when you are sitting facing north.

Moon Phase

This spell will work best if cast during the **full phase** of the Moon because you are trying to bring something to a fullness, a clarity as the Moon moves to fullness and clarity.

Day of the Week

The most favorable days of the week to cast this spell would be on **Sunday, Monday,** or **Thursday,** but it could be performed on any day of the week.

Optional Magickal Enhancements

The following items will add a deeper dimension to your spell and help you to focus yourself more fully, but they are not necessary and the spell can be cast even if you don't have these items available.

Gemstones

The best gemstones to use for this spell are **amethyst, moonstone,** and **clear quartz crystal.** If using additional gemstones other than those recommended in your formation, place them in front of you.

Incense

Incense that will enhance this spell would be **frankincense, clove,** and **pine.** Place incense in a safe place within your formation; however, light the incense outside your formation.

Music

If you like music and will not find it distracting, you might want to play something instrumental that is **meditative** and **peaceful,** like sounds of nature. Whatever you are comfortable with will be best.

Before You Start Your Spell

Make sure you have no distractions.
Turn phones off if possible.
Play soothing music.
Keep the lights dim.
Wash your hands or shower before you begin.
Gather everything you need and have it close at hand.
Draw your formation.
Ask your higher power to allow the information to flow through you.

Affirmation

Affirmation to be read within your formation *before you actually begin your spell.*

I willingly open my mind to the growth of my psychic abilities and I am invoking power within to enhance my life for good and positive purposes. May my intuition reach its highest expression. I affirm my oneness with the universal life force. I will pay close attention to messages I receive. I will examine my hunches to see how accurate I am. Surround me with the additional vibrations that are required to reach my psychic potential.

AND SO IT IS.

How to Perform the Spell

1. Light your candles, but not the incense.
2. Ring the bell and say, "I hear the power." (If two, the woman should ring the bell.)
3. Take a sip of your wine and say, "I taste the power." (If two, the man drinks first and says, "I taste the power," passes the chalice to the woman, and she repeats, "I taste the power.")
4. Light your incense or smell the fragrance of your perfume or cologne from the bottle and say, "I smell the power." (If two, the woman should light the incense.)
5. Close your eyes for a few seconds and upon opening them say, "I see the power."
6. Take your cloth and press it between your hands and say, "I feel the power."

(If two, both the man and woman should have their own separate pieces of cloth in which to hold their own energies.)

Now recite the following incantation:

With earth and air and water and fire,
My strength increases to realms much higher.
I invoke the power here tonight,
I've heard the call, it is my right.

If alone, stretch your arms out to the sky and say, "I am the power."

If two, hold hands and stretch out to the sky and say, "I am the power" (all four arms will be outstretched).

Ending incantation:

All for good, harm to none,
Now I claim this spell is done!

Conclude with any statement that signifies closure of the ceremony in your mind such as, "And so it is," "Blessed be," or "Amen." Now extinguish your candles and release your formation.

Take another sip of wine in celebration and sit in your circle for a while and reflect or perform some type of magick if you like. Perhaps reading cards of divination, crystal gazing, or working with magickal tools you enjoy. Good luck!

Making a Decision—A Pendulum Spell

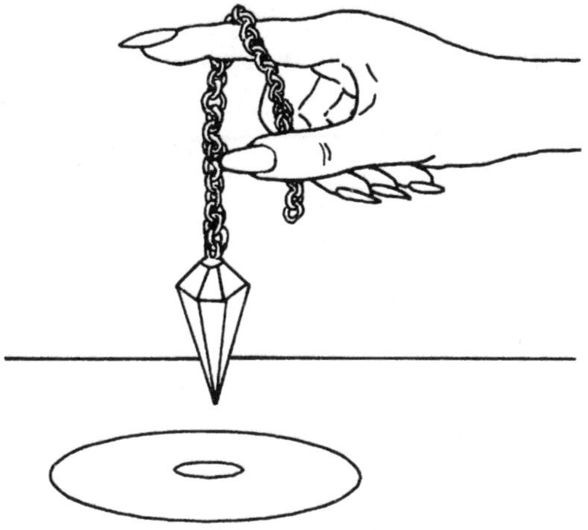

About the Pendulum

For our purposes in this publication, the pendulum is used for receiving "yes" and "no" answers from your inner self or subconscious mind, aiding you to make decisions and obtain clarity. However, this is only one use of a pendulum. People use pendulums for other purposes above and beyond answers. Healers often use pendulums to find imbalances in the physical and etheric body.

One can perform *dowsing*, which is an old art of searching for things that may be hidden, such as water or metal. Dowsing with a pendulum can also be used to locate people or objects. When I lose something in my house, I take out one of my pendulums and ask it where the lost item is. It points in the direction of the lost piece and, for the most part, it has been mystically accurate. If I cannot find the article within the house, I stand by a window. If it points in the direction of the window, I know it is outside.

It is also excellent for getting insights as to whether someone is telling you the truth about a given situation. Its ultimate purpose is to be used for questions pertaining to the present, not the future.

You can use this device alone or with another person. If you are helping another to receive answers, your subconscious will telepathically pick up the other person's subconscious mind.

Examples of the type of questions that are suited for pendulum use are:

- I don't know if the man I am seeing is serious about our relationship—is he?
- Should I move out of the place I am living?
- Will I be happy if I take that other job offer?
- Would it be beneficial for me to start this new venture?
- Should I be following a more spiritual path at this time in my life?

Remember, use only yes or no questions.

Remember that you are tapping into your subconscious to find out what you really want in life and what will lead to true happiness and fulfillment on all levels. The pendulum is such a wealth of information about present situations, events, and general decision making, you will feel great relief. You will not have to obsess about people and choices.

To sum it up, use your pendulum when you can't decide what to do about something or when you want to know if someone is telling you the whole story about a situation. If you do ask a question about the future, the pendulum will only tell you what your subconscious *wants* to happen, not what *will* happen, and you may be disappointed. Use it properly and you will see its great value and potential.

Protect This Magickal Tool

When not using your pendulum, keep it in a pouch or in some other container. It is not good to leave it exposed to other energies or vibrations. Wash your pendulum with cold water every now and then to clear it and remove vibrations from the last session. I recommend clearing or washing it when you feel it is starting to get chaotic, heavy, or you are picking up uneasy energy, but use your own intuition.

Some people never cleanse their pendulums as they feel it becomes more filled with their own vibrations with each use, therefore becoming more powerful. If someone else borrows it, make sure to clear it after they have used it by washing it or letting it clear in the light of the Sun or the Moon (new, waxing, or full).

Working with another person or people is fine as long as everyone is focused on the same question and not concerned about what they will ask when it is their turn. Having others involved can be very exciting and interesting. However, solitary use is recommended for really serious matters. Try both and see what works for you.

Some people ask if it is better to work outside or inside. It is up to you. However, I must tell you the night of a full Moon is incredible!

The pendulum just really "sings." You don't have to sit outside on the full Moon . . . just feel the energy.

Making a Pendulum

You can very inexpensively purchase a pendulum at a New Age gift store or Internet site, or you can make your own. It is basically a device consisting of a weighted object that is suspended by a string or chain above a target or fixed point (see illustration on page 195) that swings back and forth under the influence of gravity.

They are often made of gemstones, like amethyst or clear quartz crystal, as well as glass, wood, brass, and other metals. You can convert a necklace with a pointed gemstone to use as a pendulum. You may decide to use a cross, ring, or cork (wide side up) that is attached to a single chain or string.

Necessary Enhancements and Magickal Tools

The necessary tools for this spell include any tools you have chosen for your formation as described below.

- a pendulum
- a piece of paper or cardboard with a circle drawn on it (This is used as a target.)

Utilize anything that will represent a defined target and can be set flat on a table or floor. I have seen the use of quarters, buttons, or even the holes of a compact disk!)

Candles

You will also need three candles: one **white** and **two purple.** Place the white candle at the center point of the triangle in front of you and your target and the other two behind you in either corner of the triangle.

Formation

All spells should begin with casting a circle, which is your shield of protection. If you are using a triangle or a square, cast your circle first and then cast your formation within it.

The best formation for this spell is the **triangle.** Cast your formation using methods described in Chapter 5 of the book using a wand, a knife, an extended arm with fingers pointed, salt, or other material items you may have chosen.

Direction to Face

This spell is most effective if you are facing **north.** Arrange your candles as stated above and any tools or enhancements that will be in your formation so that they will be in front of you when you are sitting facing north.

Moon Phase

This spell will work best if cast during the **full** or **waxing phase** of the Moon because you are trying to bring something to a fullness, a clarity as the Moon moves to fullness and clarity.

Day of the Week

The most favorable days of the week to cast this spell would be on **Sunday** or **Monday,** but it could be performed on any day of the week.

Optional Magickal Enhancements

The following items will add a deeper dimension to your spell and help you to focus yourself more fully, but they are not necessary and the spell can be cast even if you don't have these items available.

Gemstones

The best gemstones to use for this spell are **amethyst** and **clear**

quartz crystal. If using additional gemstones other than those recommended in your formation, place them in front of you.

Incense

Incense that will enhance this spell would be **frankincense, jasmine,** and **sage.** Place incense in a safe place within your formation if you like; however, start the incense outside of your formation.

Music

If you like music and will not find it distracting, you might want to play something instrumental that is low frequency, **peaceful,** and **soothing.** Whatever you are comfortable with will be best.

Before You Start Your Pendulum Session

Make sure you have no distractions.
Turn phones off if possible.
Play soothing music.
Keep the lights dim.
Wash your hands or shower before you begin.
Light incense if you are using it.
Gather everything you need and have it close at hand.
Draw your formation.

Now is the time to light the candles. If using two candles, place one on each side of the target card. If using three candles, create a triangle around you (if sitting on the floor), or create a triangle with candles in front of you on a table or platform. There is power in threes. The point of the triangle should be in front of you.

Ask your higher power to allow the information to flow through you.

How to Use Your Pendulum to Obtain Yes/No Answers

Place your target card in front of you.

Hold the pendulum suspended from *one hand* with the point approximately one inch above the center circle on your target card. You can bend your elbow or keep your arm straight; it's easier to bend your elbow. "Still" the pendulum so it is not moving. Sometimes saying something like "quiet," "still," or "stay" works. You can say this aloud or to yourself.

Once you have gotten the pendulum to stay still, you will now determine what direction yes and no are. This will be different every time. Hence, I do not put yes or no directions on the target card.

Ask a question you know the answer to must be yes, such as, "Is my name ______?" If you gave your real name, it will point in the direction that will now determine yes.

Next, ask a question you know is a no answer. This should swing in the opposite direction of yes. If it does not, try again until you get clear directions for yes and no.

Now you have determined the direction of yes and no for this particular day or night. Your directions may change daily, so do this procedure each time. It is not necessary to do it after each question—just every twenty-four hours or more.

Once you go through this setup procedure, you can ask all the questions you want. (However, don't go overboard!) If you find the needle of the pendulum is going in circles or in a direction that makes no sense, stop and start over. If it still continues, put it away and attempt again on another day. For the most part, you should not encounter that problem.

If you notice your hand shakes or moves a bit, don't be concerned. Your subconscious motivates the brain to send a type of electrical impulse to your hand, therefore moving the pendulum. Remember, this is a device to help you get in touch with your subconscious. If you want one thing and the pendulum tells you something different, you need to think about the message your inner self is trying to convey.

Example: The man I have been dating for three years is a "free spirit" who does not like to work, has no ambition, uses me, and I think sees other women on occasion. However, I still love him and I can't help it. Will he change and is he the one for me?

If you want the pendulum to say yes and it says no, consider the reason for the different point of view. Maybe there is something you're not admitting and you need to deal with it. *I think you get the point!*

Conclude with any statement that signifies closure of the ceremony in your mind such as, "And so it is," "Blessed be," or "Amen." Now extinguish your candles and release your formation.

Prosperity

Necessary Enhancements and Magickal Tools

The necessary tools for this spell include any tools you have chosen for your formation as described below.

You will need:

- your wallet
- a key that opens nothing (Go to a hardware store or a place that sells blank keys and purchase a gold-colored key. If the clerk thinks this is strange, do not go into detail about the fact that you want it for a spell. Keep your business to

yourself as this strengthens any spell. And remember that it must be a new key. Do not use an old key you have lying around the house.)

Candles

You will also need **four green** candles set on the sides of your square formation so that one is east, west, north, and south.

Formation

All spells should begin with casting a circle, which is your shield of protection. If you are using a triangle or a square, cast your circle first and then cast your formation within it.

The best formation for this spell is the **square.** Cast your formation using methods described in Chapter 5 of the book using a wand, a knife, an extended arm with fingers pointed, salt, or other material items you may have chosen.

Direction to Face

This spell is most effective if you are facing **east.** Arrange your candles as stated above and any tools or enhancements that will be in your formation so that they will be in front of you when you are sitting facing east.

Moon Phase

This spell will work best if cast during the **full, new,** or **waxing phase** of the Moon because you are trying increase something as the Moon increases to fullness.

Day of the Week

The most favorable days of the week to cast this spell would be on **Sunday, Wednesday,** and **Thursday.**

Optional Magickal Enhancements

The following items will add a deeper dimension to your spell and help you to focus yourself more fully, but they are not necessary and the spell can be cast even if you don't have these items available.

Gemstones

The best gemstones to use for this spell are **pyrite, green tourmaline,** and **clear quartz crystal.** If using additional gemstones other than those recommended in your formation, place them in front of you.

Incense

Incense that will enhance this spell would be **vanilla, mint,** and **allspice.** Place incense in a safe place within your formation if you like; however, start the incense outside of your formation.

Music

If you like music and will not find it distracting, you might want to play something instrumental that is **uplifting.** Whatever you are comfortable with will be best.

Before You Start Your Spell

Make sure you have no distractions.
Turn phones off if possible.
Play soothing music.
Keep the lights dim.
Wash your hands or shower before you begin.
Light incense if you are using it.
Gather everything you need and have it close at hand.
Draw your formation.

Ask your higher power to allow the information to flow through you. Light the three candles that are not in front of you.

Affirmation

Affirmation to be read within your formation *before you actually begin your spell.*

I give myself permission to allow for financial security. I let go of any obstacles that block my path. I know you need not live a life of poverty to find spiritual fulfillment.

I release any thoughts that make me feel unworthy of a prosperous lifestyle. May abundance and prosperity resonate to me starting this moment.

AND SO IT IS.

How to Perform the Spell

Take your key and use it as a tool to carve on the side of the green candle in front of you the word "Prosperity."

Light the candle.

Take the key and place it in your wallet.

Now recite the following incantation:

The earth, the wind, the Sun, the sea,
Put magick in this special key.
My money growing with the Moon,
Prosperity cometh and be here soon.

Conclude with any statement that signifies closure of the ceremony in your mind such as "And so it is," "Blessed be," or "Amen." Now extinguish your candles and release your formation.

Safe Travel

This spell takes two days or more, weather permitting, and will be done in two parts.

The best time to do this spell is when the weather will be clear and fair.

Necessary Enhancements and Magickal Tools

The necessary tools for this spell include any tools you have chosen for your formation as described below.

You will need:

- a talisman (This can be any charm or gemstone that means something to you that can be worn on a chain. You may use a cross, pentagram, crystal, or even an animal fetish. You may have a necklace that you already wear which you can also use by programming it.
- element water
- bowl, cup, or chalice that will hold your talisman.

Candles

You will also need three candles for the first day: **silver/gray, brown,** and **red.** Set them in a row in front of you with the silver/gray to the left, the brown in the middle, and the red to the right. The second day you will need one **white** candle set in front of you.

Formation

All spells should begin with casting a circle, which is your shield of protection. If you are using a triangle or a square, cast your circle first and then cast your formation within it.

The best formation for this spell is the **circle.** Cast your formation using methods described in Chapter 5 of the book using a wand, a knife, an extended arm with fingers pointed, salt, or other material items you may have chosen.

Direction to Face

This spell is most effective if you are facing **north.** Arrange your candles as stated above and any tools or enhancements that will be in your formation so that they will be in front of you when you are sitting facing north.

Moon Phase

This spell will work best if cast during the **new** or **waxing phase** of the Moon because you are trying to increase something as the Moon increases to fullness.

Day of the Week

Cast this spell on **any day** of the week.

Optional Magickal Enhancements

The following items will add a deeper dimension to your spell and help you to focus yourself more fully, but they are not necessary and the spell can be cast even if you don't have these items available.

Gemstones

The best gemstones to use for this spell are **turquoise** and **tiger's eye.** If using additional gemstones other than those recommended in your formation, place them in front of you.

Incense

Incense that will enhance this spell would **be sandalwood, cinnamon,** and **lavender.** Place incense in a safe place within your formation if you like; however, start the incense outside of your formation.

Music

If you like music and will not find it distracting, you might want to play something instrumental that is **quiet** and **soothing.** Whatever you are comfortable with will be best.

Before You Start Your Spell

Make sure you have no distractions.
Turn phones off if possible.
Play soothing music.
Keep the lights dim.
Wash your hands or shower before you begin.
Light incense if you are using it.
Gather everything you need and have it close at hand.
Draw your formation.
Ask your higher power to allow the information to flow through you.

Affirmation

Affirmation to be read within your formation *before you actually begin your spell.*

The feeling of safety and security when I travel is of tremendous importance to me. The thought of having that extra degree of protection is of great comfort when taking a trip, whether it is long or short. I know (fill in the name of the God or higher power you pray to) will protect me, whether I am active during the day or sleeping at night.

I have peace in knowing I am being looked after with love and good intentions.

How to Perform the Spell

Part 1: First you will cast magick into your charm, thereby creating a talisman:

Take your charm or gemstone and set it in the bowl.

Pour your element water over the charm so it is totally covered.

Place your hand over the dish, but not touching it, with palms down and say, "May the elements that created this water now charge this charm with the powers of protection."

Now disperse your circle, extinguish your candles, and say, "So all is done for now."

Set the talisman on a windowsill, deck, or somewhere inside or outside where the Sun and the Moon can energize it. This should take at least twenty-four hours. You need moonlight and sunlight—cloudy days will not do. If you should have weather that is not conducive, you must leave the charm exposed until it has at least eight hours of sunlight and eight hours of moonlight. Better too much than not enough. If it rains a little, do not be concerned.

Part 2: The next possible day after you feel your talisman has been sufficiently charged by the Sun and the Moon, leave your talisman in the water and cast your circle again.

Light a white candle, and put your talisman in front of you and leave it sitting in the water.

Now recite the following incantation:

Nature herself has blessed this piece,
My safety sure, all fears released.
I keep this amulet strong and clear,
I travel safely throughout the year.

Conclude with any statement that signifies closure of the ceremony in your mind such as "And so it is," "Blessed be," or "Amen."

Now extinguish your candle and release your formation.

You may wear this when traveling only, every day, or when you just need to. This is your choice. Perform this spell once a year if keeping the same charm or crystal.

Special Intentions

This spell is meant to provide for all the spells that are not included in this book. Put in your own intention.

Necessary Enhancements and Magickal Tools

The necessary tools for this spell include any tools you have chosen for your formation as described below.

Candles

You will need one **white** candle.

Formation

All spells should begin with casting a circle, which is your shield of protection. If you are using a triangle or a square, cast your circle first and then cast your formation within it.

The best formation for this spell is the **circle.** Cast your formation using methods described in Chapter 5 of the book using a wand, a knife, an extended arm with fingers pointed, salt, or other material items you may have chosen.

Direction to Face

This spell is most effective if you are facing **north.** Arrange your candles as stated above and any tools or enhancements that will be in your formation so that they will be in front of you when you are sitting facing north.

Moon Phase

This spell will work best if cast during the **full, new,** or **waxing phase** of the Moon.

Day of the Week

Cast this spell on **any day** of the week.

Optional Magickal Enhancements

The following items will add a deeper dimension to your spell and help you to focus yourself more fully, but they are not necessary and the spell can be cast even if you don't have these items available.

Gemstones

The best gemstone to use for this spell is **clear quartz crystal.** If using additional gemstones other than those recommended in your formation, place them in front of you.

Incense

Incense that will enhance this spell would be **jasmine.** Place incense in a safe place within your formation if you like; however, start the incense outside of your formation.

Music

If you like music and will not find it distracting, you might want to play something **classical, acoustic,** or **New Age.** Whatever you are comfortable with will be best.

Before You Start Your Spell

Make sure you have no distractions.

Turn phones off if possible.

Play soothing music.

Keep the lights dim.

Wash your hands or shower before you begin.

Light incense if you are using it.

Gather everything you need and have it close at hand.

Draw your formation.

Ask your higher power to allow the information to flow through you.

Affirmation

Affirmation to be read within your formation *before you actually begin your spell.*

I direct my energy tonight to one specific desire. That desire is . . . (state your desire).

The power is available to bring this into being. I thank the resource from which it comes.

May messages regarding this special intention flood my consciousness; I carry myself with confidence, knowing that the divine will do what is best for me in this situation. Allow this to come into fruition.

How to Perform the Spell

Say out loud or to yourself: "Within the authority of the highest ability in the universal force, I ask that . . . (fill in your request). Thank you and so it is.

Now recite the following incantation:

Moon, oh, Moon, hear my desire,
Earth to water, wind to fire,

I ask it once and three times three,
Bring my request in harmony.

Conclude with any statement that signifies closure of the ceremony in your mind such as "And so it is," "Blessed be," or "Amen." Now extinguish your candles and release your formation.

White Light Protection Spell

As stated earlier in the book, before you cast any spell, you should protect yourself and your formation with white light. This still holds true. However, this is a special spell that goes beyond that protection. Cast this spell when you are frightened or when you want to keep someone or something away from you. This can refer to living and nonliving entities as well. It can include gossip, bad luck, the loss of money, or any negativity you think is going to come into your life or is already there.

This is a strong and powerful spell, so I will elaborate further for the purpose behind the requirements.

The reason the circle is the best choice is because the circle formation will not allow anything to drift back into it, as the circle protects all from re-entering.

You face the direction east because the vibration of the east is that of new beginnings and building powers. The Sun rises in the east. It replaces the darkness.

Necessary Enhancements and Magickal Tools

The necessary tools for this spell include any tools you have chosen for your formation as described below.

Candles

You will need **three white** candles set in front of you in a row.

Formation

All spells should begin with casting a circle, which is your shield of protection. If you are using a triangle or a square, cast your circle first and then cast your formation within it.

The best formation for this spell is the **circle.** Cast your formation using methods described in Chapter 5 of the book using a wand, a knife, an extended arm with fingers pointed, salt, or other material items you may have chosen.

Direction to Face

This spell is most effective if you are facing **east.** Arrange your candles as stated above and any tools or enhancements that will be in your formation so that they will be in front of you when you are sitting facing east.

Moon Phase

This spell will work best if cast during the **dark** or **waning phase** of the Moon, as this is a form of banishing.

Day of the Week

Cast this spell on **any day** of the week.

Optional Magickal Enhancements

The following items will add a deeper dimension to your spell and help you to focus yourself more fully, but they are not necessary and the spell can be cast even if you don't have these items available.

Gemstones

The best gemstone to use for this spell is **obsidian.** If using additional gemstones other than those recommended in your formation, place them in front of you.

Incense

Incense that will enhance this spell would be **frankincense.** Place incense in a safe place within your formation if you like; however, start the incense outside of your formation.

Music

If you like music and will not find it distracting, you might want to play something **classical, acoustic,** or **New Age.** Whatever you are comfortable with will be best.

Before You Start Your Spell

Make sure you have no distractions.
Turn phones off if possible.
Play soothing music.
Keep the lights dim.
Wash your hands or shower before you begin.
Light incense if you are using it.
Gather everything you need and have it close at hand.
Draw your formation.
Ask your higher power to allow the information to flow through you.

How to Perform the Spell

As you sit in your circle formation, visualize a circle of light surrounding you from the ground through the roof and into the sky, encompassing your spell area and rising into the cosmos where no one can reach. Hold this visualization of this engulfing white light for a few seconds. Then relax and see the circle dissipate. The potency of its light will still remain.

Now recite the following incantation:

This light of protection I carry it strong,
No ill wishes or trouble can now come along.
You cannot harm me or weaken my soul,
My light is my weapon and peace is my goal.

Conclude with any statement that signifies closure of the ceremony in your mind such as "And so it is," "Blessed be," or "Amen." Now extinguish your candles and release your formation.

Renew this white light protection spell at least every week or sooner if you feel you are in need of special assistance at a difficult time in your life.

PART IV
Lanterns of Light

Monday's child is fair of face,
Tuesday's child is full of grace,
Wednesday's child is full of woe,
Thursday's child has far to go,
Friday's child is loving and giving,
Saturday's child works hard for its living,
And a child born on the Sabbath day
Is fair and wise and good and gay.

—Unknown

Introduction

The following additional related topics are general guides to give you a better understanding of certain characteristics you may possess. These are what I think of as "additional lights" that can assist in guiding you down your pathway in life.

Although this is fun and fascinating information, understand these are the simplest and most basic forms of these systems. Further investigation of these subjects may provide for you a new interest or pastime. Please take a look and see what you think. Remember, if you keep your eyes shut, what good is the light?

19

Chinese Astrology

Chinese astrology refers to twelve animals representing a twelve-year cycle based on the lunar calendar. They use these zodiac animals as a structure to depict a person's character and their very nature according to the year in which they were born.

To discover what animal sign represents you, see the list below. Simply find your year of birth and the corresponding animal. The characteristics of these animals are said to represent some of your main personality traits.

Also, you will see an element listed with each year. By applying the elements, we can see differences between two people of the same animal sign but born in different years. Example: Someone born in 1960 is a Rat and their element is Metal, making him or her a Metal Rat. While someone born in the year 1948 is also a Rat, his or her element sign is Earth. These two people have commonalities, yet there are still subtle differences.

Chinese Astrology Year Chart

YEAR	ANIMAL SYMBOL	ELEMENT	YEAR	ANIMAL SYMBOL	ELEMENT	YEAR	ANIMAL SYMBOL	ELEMENT
1900	Rat	Metal	1936	Rat	Fire	1972	Rat	Water
1901	Ox	Metal	1937	Ox	Fire	1973	Ox	Water
1902	Tiger	Water	1938	Tiger	Earth	1974	Tiger	Wood
1903	Rabbit	Water	1939	Rabbit	Earth	1975	Rabbit	Wood
1904	Dragon	Wood	1940	Dragon	Metal	1976	Dragon	Fire
1905	Snake	Wood	1941	Snake	Metal	1977	Snake	Fire
1906	Horse	Fire	1942	Horse	Water	1978	Horse	Earth
1907	Sheep	Fire	1943	Sheep	Water	1979	Sheep	Earth
1908	Monkey	Earth	1944	Monkey	Wood	1980	Monkey	Metal
1909	Rooster	Earth	1945	Rooster	Wood	1981	Rooster	Metal
1910	Dog	Metal	1946	Dog	Fire	1982	Dog	Water
1911	Pig	Metal	1947	Pig	Fire	1983	Pig	Water
1912	Rat	Water	1948	Rat	Earth	1984	Rat	Wood
1913	Ox	Water	1949	Ox	Earth	1985	Ox	Wood
1914	Tiger	Wood	1950	Tiger	Metal	1986	Tiger	Fire
1915	Rabbit	Wood	1951	Rabbit	Metal	1987	Rabbit	Fire
1916	Dragon	Fire	1952	Dragon	Water	1988	Dragon	Earth
1917	Snake	Fire	1953	Snake	Water	1989	Snake	Earth
1918	Horse	Earth	1954	Horse	Wood	1990	Horse	Metal
1919	Sheep	Earth	1955	Sheep	Wood	1991	Sheep	Metal
1920	Monkey	Metal	1956	Monkey	Fire	1992	Monkey	Water
1921	Rooster	Metal	1957	Rooster	Fire	1993	Rooster	Water
1922	Dog	Water	1958	Dog	Earth	1994	Dog	Wood

Chinese Astrology Year Chart *(continued)*

YEAR	ANIMAL SYMBOL	ELEMENT	YEAR	ANIMAL SYMBOL	ELEMENT	YEAR	ANIMAL SYMBOL	ELEMENT
1923	Pig	Water	1959	Pig	Earth	1995	Pig	Wood
1924	Rat	Wood	1960	Rat	Metal	1996	Rat	Fire
1925	Ox	Wood	1961	Ox	Metal	1997	Ox	Fire
1926	Tiger	Fire	1962	Tiger	Water	1998	Tiger	Earth
1927	Rabbit	Fire	1963	Rabbit	Water	1999	Rabbit	Earth
1928	Dragon	Earth	1964	Dragon	Wood	2000	Dragon	Metal
1929	Snake	Earth	1965	Snake	Wood	2001	Snake	Metal
1930	Horse	Metal	1966	Horse	Fire	2002	Horse	Water
1931	Sheep	Metal	1967	Sheep	Fire	2003	Sheep	Water
1932	Monkey	Water	1968	Monkey	Earth	2004	Monkey	Wood
1933	Rooster	Water	1969	Rooster	Earth	2005	Rooster	Wood
1934	Dog	Wood	1970	Dog	Metal	2006	Dog	Fire
1935	Pig	Wood	1971	Pig	Metal	2007	Pig	Fire

The Characteristics of the Animal Zodiac Signs/Chinese Astrology

The Rat: Charm and Intelligence

Those born under the influence of the Rat are also dynamic and usually have active lives. They exhibit extremes when it comes to money matters, being too generous at times and too frugal at other times. Rats are not couch potatoes and love adventure and thrill seeking. They have great control over their romantic feelings yet are highly sensual once you get to know them.

The Ox: Enterprise and Stability

Those born under the influence of the Ox have much common sense and are very practical. They are not against hard work and will strive until they reach their goals. They are faithful and fall in love slowly, expecting their partners to do the same.

The Tiger: Bravery and Protection

Those born under the influence of the Tiger tend to attract people and are always ready to fight for a just cause. They create their own reality and like to do things their way. They can tend to be flirtatious and filled with eroticism.

The Rabbit: Humbleness and Family Life

Those born under the influence of the Rabbit are extremely good-natured. Because of their sensitive nature, you will find many Rabbits in the creative fields. Rabbits do not like to argue and will tend to mate with easygoing people.

The Dragon: Luck and Good Fortune

Those born under the influence of the Dragon can fit in with almost any type of crowd or situation. The opposite sex is extremely drawn to the Dragon. While the Dragon has strong physical attractions, an individual's intelligence can be just as stimulating to them, as well.

The Snake: Wisdom and Wit

Those born under the influence of the Snake are mystical and mysterious. They are excellent with money matters and seem to live charmed lives. They are mostly above-average in physical appearance and look for a mate that is above-average in all areas. Success and power are turn-ons for most Snakes.

The Horse: Refinement and Eagerness

Those born under the influence of the Horse tend to have many friends and a sense of humor, as well as being enthusiastic and learning quickly. When you meet a Horse for the first time, you may feel as if you have known him or her for years. Love can make the normally practical Horse be disposed to not thinking clearly. They also tend to fall in love too easily and often settle down later in life.

The Sheep: The Arts and Sensitivity

Those born under the influence of the Sheep are peaceful people. They do not want to cause undue problems or chaos. They are mostly team players and would rather be part of a group than working on their own. Sheep love their home and would rather be married or in a partnership than single. Sheep by nature are affectionate and love to be loved.

The Monkey: Imagination and Popularity

Those born under the influence of Monkey are inventive and can come to correct conclusions about people, places, and things immediately. The Monkey has a tendency to get bored quickly, which causes them to change romantic partners often. However, once they decide to finally settle down, they make intriguing and exciting partners.

The Rooster: Flamboyance and Confidence

Those born under the influence of the Rooster are very organized and have control over their business affairs. They love attention and enjoy entertaining. Roosters will be faithful once they find someone with whom they are truly happy. However, this could take them some time as they can alienate a potentially good partner with their sometimes critical remarks. Because they pride themselves on their honesty, they are usually monogamous in relationships and never "kiss and tell."

The Dog: Loyalty and Protection

Those born under the influence of the Dog are great humanitarians. They will lend a hand to a friend or stranger in times of need and look for nothing in return. This sign is not materialistic, and they put a loving partner above all things. Once they find their romantic match, they will stay with their partner through sunshine and storms.

The Pig: Honesty and Harmony

Those born under the influence of the Pig love to be surrounded by beautiful things.

They love to live in the height of luxury and feel they are well worth it. They don't mind working hard and getting their hands dirty, but in return they will indulge themselves in a reward. The entertaining they do is "all or nothing." They throw out the red carpet for their friends. Pigs do not allow their sexual desires go unattended. They immensely enjoy the gratification of their intimate partner and are devoted to the ones they love.

Meanings of the Elements/Chinese Astrology

Metal

Positive aspects of your personality: Determination, flare for speaking, being self-assured, powerful and energized disposition. A self-made person.

Aspects that need some transformation: Stubborn attitude, not always being reasonable and using common sense.

Message from your path of evolution: "Lighten up and think about what others have to say. You will not lose strength but only gain respect from others for listening to both sides."

Wood

Positive aspects of your personality: Being creative and artistic, a moral individual, unselfish and compassionate, adventuresome and always willing to learn.

Aspects that need some transformation: Too idealistic, passive.

Message from your path of evolution: "Finish what you start. Stay constant and do not jump from one project to the other unless they can all be accomplished successfully."

Water

Positive aspects of your personality: Total sensitivity to its highest degree. You are a thinker and a diplomat, persuasive in a gentle yet firm way.

You "get it" as far as understanding how people think and what their needs are.

Aspects that need some transformation: Overly patient. Don't wait too long before you let your voice be heard.

Message from your path of evolution: "Don't let emotions cloud your common sense. Do what is best for you and it will most likely be what is best for everyone involved. Be a little selfish and it will work with you, not against you."

Fire

Positive aspects of your personality: Leadership, "movers and shakers," passionate and aggressive, totally confident, excellent communication skills.

Aspects that need some transformation: Sometimes self-serving, impatient, and not understanding of others' points of view, as well as a possible workaholic.

Message from your path of evolution: "Be composed. Stop and smell the roses. Use your fiery passion for love . . . not just business."

Earth

Positive aspects of your personality: Wisdom, stability, logical nature, and reliability. Industrious and serious money-making abilities. Unspoken sexuality in the most primitive sense.

Aspects that need some transformation: Lack of imagination at times, a creative nature that is hidden because you feel you have not earned the right to relax yet in life.

Message from your path of evolution: "Get a little wild! Do something that is not like you and is not predictable. Tell people you care about how you really feel."

Chinese Zodiac Compatibility Chart

This chart will show you the animal symbols of the zodiac with whom you are most likely to get along well.

ANIMAL SYMBOL	COMPATIBLE ANIMALS	ANIMALS TO AVOID
Rat	Dragons and Monkeys	Horses
Ox	Snakes and Roosters	Sheep
Tiger	Horses and Dogs	Monkeys
Rabbit	Sheep and Pigs	Roosters
Dragon	Monkeys and Rats	Dogs
Snakes	Roosters and Oxen	Boars
Horse	Tigers and Dogs	Rats
Sheep	Boars and Rabbits	Oxen
Monkey	Dragons and Rats	Tigers
Rooster	Snakes and Oxen	Rabbits
Dog	Horses and Tigers	Dragons
Pig	Rabbits and Sheep	other Pigs

Note: Different traditions may use different names for some animal symbols. For example, oxen are sometimes described as buffalos, rabbits as cats, sheep as goats, pigs as boars, and roosters as cocks.

20

Numerology

Numerology is the study of the meanings of numbers. Each number is said to have a special vibration, which equates to a different message and definition. The most common starting point in numerology is to add together the numbers from your date of birth and reduce them to a single digit for the purpose of revealing your path of life. Each number has a special meaning and gives you insights and direction. Pay attention and you may be surprised how accurate numerology can be.

Numerology goes beyond solely determining your path in life. It can also assist you in determining such things as where to live from a mere street address. You can also use your name to garner further information about your life.

Numerology is simple to learn, and after a while, you may find yourself adding up numbers on everything numerical you come across. One can add up the number of a motel room to test whether or not they will have a good time or unusual happenings. You can total dates and phone numbers or anything you choose. Numerology is fun and something that can be learned quickly for your personal use. Of course, to be a professional numerologist, as with anything, it requires more time and study of the vibrations of numbers.

How to Find Your Life Path/Destiny Number

The basic idea is to calculate your date of birth down to one single number or digit.

There are two exceptions to this rule. If the sum of your date of birth should add up to 11 or 22, they stand as they are. They are not further reduced because these are considered master numbers.

You first add together the number of the month you were born, add it to the calendar day number you were born, and then to the year you were born. You should have a four-digit number. Add these four digits together to get a two-digit number. Lastly, add the two-digit number (unless it is 11 or 22), and you will come up with a single-digit number, which is your life path number.

Example: Mary Jones was born on May 15, 1958, which is numerically 5/15/1958 and will be added like this:

Month of birth: 5
Day of birth: 15
Year of birth: 1958
Total: 1978

Reduce these numbers further by adding them separately:
1 + 9 + 7 + 8 = 25
Now reduce the last number, 25, to find a single number:
2 + 5 = 7
Mary Jones's life path number is 7.

Example of an exception: John Smith was born on January 29, 1963, which numerically is 1/29/1963 and will be added like this:

Month of birth: 1
Day of birth: 29
Year of birth: 1963
Total: 1993

Reduce these numbers further by adding them separately:
1 + 9 + 9 + 3 = 22

The number is 22 is a master number, so in this case you leave it at 22. Remember, only 22 and 11 are exceptions; all other numbers would be added further to arrive at a one-digit number.

Number Interpretations

These number definitions are the standard interpretations.

1 (One)

Personal interpretation: One represents individuality. This is the number of a trailblazer and pathfinder. You lead and do not follow, doing better in your own business as opposed to working for someone else. Ones are self-sufficient and honest and have a natural flare for inventions. People that vibrate to this number always finish their plans or projects.

General interpretation: Positive aspects—independence, unity, new beginnings, organization, creativity, unconventionality, communicative. Negatives aspects—laziness, selfishness, overly aggressive.

2 (Two)

Personal interpretation: Two represents joint action. You are a team player and do not like working or living alone. You enjoy community work and give without expecting anything in return. You are the peacemakers of the world and are loved for your kindness and good will. Twos can be shy at times and would rather live with someone than live alone.

General interpretation: Positive aspects—cooperation, diplomacy, duality, gentleness, security, kindness and love, patience. Negative aspects—too passive, overly self-supportive, hypersensitivity.

3 (Three)

Personal interpretation: Three represents creativity. You are popular and work better mentally than physically. You are the writers, artists, and musicians in the world. Kindness and intuition best describe your nature. You bring happiness to others and love to build and create. You follow your dreams and achieve them. You enjoy nature and see the beauty in all things.

General interpretation: Positive aspects—enthusiasm, imagination, creativity, leadership, talent, merriment, sexuality, inspirational. Negative aspects—jealousy, overexpectations of others.

4 (Four)

Personal interpretation: Four represents organization. You are practical, logical, and get the job done without complaining. You are a homebody and do not take foolish chances. Responsibility is your nature and everyone counts on you to make things right.

You do not like surprises and like to have everything in its place. You are an excellent provider and are the epitome of the word stable.

General interpretation: Positive aspects—organized, solid, no nonsense, industry, serious, detailed, protection, and safety. Negative aspects—overwork, impatience, boring, and stubborn.

5 (Five)

Personal interpretation: Five represents freedom. You enjoy change and do not want to be tied down to anything or anyone. You are an adventurer and "want to do it all." Fives like dealing with the public and are anxious to learn. You make friends quickly and are not apprehensive about trying new ideas. You are at no time a couch potato and like excitement in your life, so you seek it.

General interpretation: Positive aspects—change, versatility, energetic, unique, travel, the unconventional. Negative aspects—overindulgence, irresponsibility, not stable.

6 (Six)

Personal interpretation: Six represents harmony. You have an artistic nature and love family and friends. You are a giver and would rather give than receive. Sixes are responsible and humanitarians. Entertaining and sharing what you have with others is also of your nature. You are a partnership type as opposed to being a loner.

General interpretation: Positive aspects—responsibility, beauty, nature, loving, social, and security. Negative aspects—pride to a fault, interference, and stubbornness.

7 (Seven)

Personal interpretation: Seven represents understanding. You are very wise and a seeker of knowledge. You enjoy your own company and do not mind being alone and reflecting about life. Sevens lean toward metaphysics and the paranormal. Spirituality is part of your life's journey. Psychic work would well suit you and sometimes you can be misunderstood and considered a bit unusual.

General interpretation: Positive aspects—meditation, learning, professionalism, teaching, counseling, and intelligence. Negative aspects—laziness, apathy, daydreams, and addictive behavior.

8 (Eight)

Personal interpretation: Eight represents power. You are an achiever and successful. Eights figure out how the universe works and use it to get what they want in life, without being greedy once you learn balance. You have a tendency to take everything to its utmost and do not do anything halfway. Public speaking is a forte and you are a good communicator, not only verbally but also in written form.

General interpretation: Positive aspects—business, money, ambition, charity, metaphysical, accomplished. Negative aspects—extravagance, narrow-mindedness, harsh.

9 (Nine)

Personal interpretation: Nine represents completion. You are compassionate, loving, caring, and sensitive. Nines are well suited for giving intelligent advice and guidance.

You have high levels of natural intuition and are best to follow your own thoughts and feelings. You share your knowledge and insights with others as this brings you great pleasure. Forgiving and forgetting is instilled in you, for you have journeyed far above petty things.

General interpretation: Positive aspects—intuitiveness, fulfillment, peacefulness, creativity, and brilliance. Negative aspects—moodiness, occasional selfishness, and shyness.

11 (Eleven)

Personal interpretation: Eleven is a master number of illumination. You should be up on stage teaching, educating, and making a difference in the world. Elevens are philosophical and of them much is expected. You could be everything from a famous artist to a politician. The options are limitless, and you have the ability to make people think. People watch what you do and follow you, so be careful in all you do and say.

General interpretation: Positive aspects—ability, psychic knowledge, inspirational. Negative aspects—conceit, skepticism, and coolness toward others.

22 (Twenty-two)

Personal interpretation: Twenty-two is the number of self-mastery.

You are the master of any trade or profession you pursue and should use your expertise to benefit others and work on a large scale in what you have chosen. You do not open a small-town business—instead you put together a major worldwide corporation.

You do not receive a letter of recognition, but win the Pulitzer Prize. Your path is universal and expansive.

General interpretation: Positive aspects—leadership, visionary, achievement, and fame for helping others. Negative aspects—vanity, stress, and insensitiveness.

Here are a few additional quick and fun things to experiment with in numerology:

- Add up your address at your own home and see the results.

Example 438 Elm Street. Add: 4 + 3 + 8 = 15. Then, 1 + 5 = 6. If this were your address, you would simply look up the number 6 in the interpretation list and see if it pertains to the way you feel in your home or about a potential home.

- Add up the number of your motel room the next time you go on vacation.

Example: Room #91, 9 + 1 = 10. Then, 1 + 0 = 1. Look up the number 1 and see if it gives you some interesting bits of information about what kind of vacation you will have.

If a room is only one number such as 3, simply look up the number 3.

If you would like to add up the numbers in your name, refer to the alphabet below and use the same standard method. Always use your full name that is written on your birth certificate, even if you do not use it in public. If you are adopted, still use your original birth name if you know it.

The name on your birth certificate carries the strongest vibration. Do not use nicknames, stage names, married names, or anything containing Junior or Jr.

Barbara J. Bishop tells us in her book *Numerology* that the use of Junior or Jr. is "only a designation given with a name and not used in numerology." She also advises when figuring the name of a business, do not include the word *corporation, corp.,* or *inc.* as a part of the company's full name.

Alphabet and Corresponding Number Chart

1	2	3	4	5	6	7	8	9
A	B	C	D	E	F	G	H	I
J	K	L	M	N	O	P	Q	R
S	T	U	V	W	X	Y	Z	

Find the corresponding number for each letter in your name and calculate as you did with your birth date.

Example of a full name: C A R O L M A R I E J O H N S O N

Corresponding numbers: 3 1 9 6 3 4 1 9 9 5 1 6 8 5 1 6 5

Add the numbers together:

3 + 1 + 9 + 6 + 3 = 22, 4 + 1 + 9 + 9 + 5 = 28,

1 + 6 + 8 + 5 + 1 + 6 + 5 = 32

Add totals: 22 + 28 + 32 = 82

Continue to add down until you reach a single number:

8 + 2 = 10

Finally: 1 + 0 = 1

• 21 •

Western Astrology

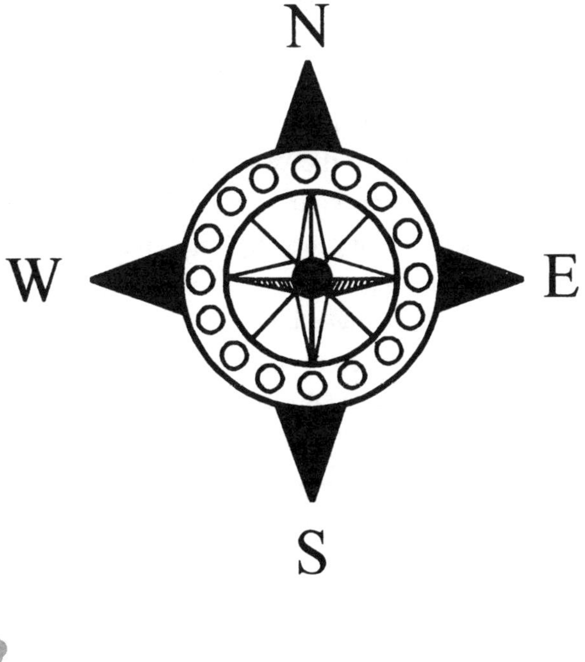

Regardless of whether or not you have a belief in Western astrology, you have most likely noticed it throughout your life. Our horoscopes are written in the daily newspapers, on the Internet, in magazines, printed on calendars, coffee cups—just about anything you can imagine. Most people, regardless of their beliefs, know which sign they are when asked. For those who do not know, they will at least know the philosophy of astrology exists. The words astrology, daily horoscopes, and zodiac signs are not foreign to them.

Western astrology is based on the Sun, unlike Eastern astrology, which is based on the Moon. Western astrology uses symbolism of planets to express our nature and character.

In this section, I have decided to include the widespread information regarding the Western zodiac and information about each sign for a quick reference. These interpretations are only the very general information of Western astrology. This is a complex subject; and to become a professional astrologer and a true expert, it takes years of study to fully understand the system.

There are twelve signs in the zodiac and a specific planet rules each. The different Sun signs of the Western zodiac depict personality traits you may have. Discover your sign by finding the month and date you were born and looking up the characteristics of your sign. The dates given may vary depending upon the source, but are generally very close to what I have given here. Also, four elements are associated with each sign and represent another aspect of the personality.

I do not elaborate extensively on Western astrology in this section because this information is readily available to the majority of readers.

Astrological Signs and Influences

Aries

(The Ram) March 21 to April 20

Ruled by: Mars
Element: Fire
Character traits: Aries people have excellent executive abilities. They

are spontaneous and generous. People within this fiery sign should guard against becoming too stubborn and must learn to control their emotional behavior. This is a creative sign, born to lead, not to follow . . . and they are good leaders.

Taurus

(The Bull) April 21 to May 20

Ruled by: Venus
Element: Earth
Character traits: Tauruses exhibit self-control and are consistent in what they do. They are true to their partners and make good parents. Hard-working and rarely ill, they are uncomplicated people and easy to get along with. They are warm, grounded, and believe in "making love, not war."

Gemini

(The Twins) May 21 to June 20

Ruled by: Mercury
Element: Air
Character traits: Geminis are charming and brilliant, passionate and detached. The Gemini is definitely a duality and loves change. Communicating with others is their forte, and they will consider both sides of any dispute before making a judgment. They catch on quickly and have inquisitive minds.

Cancer

(The Crab) June 21 to July 20

Ruled by: the Moon
Element: Water
Character traits: Cancers are sensitive and kind. They are intuitive and loving, but can be prone to worrying too much about the people they care about. Here, we also find a duality, as a Cancer can be up on stage one minute, getting attention from audiences, or living alone on a mountaintop the next.

Leo

(The Lion) July 21 to August 20

Ruled by: the Sun
Element: Fire
Character traits: Leos are born to be leaders. They are at ease in powerful positions and love to be there. They can be very generous, but forgive and forget easily. Sometimes they must learn to be a bit more humble. They will give but rarely take.

Virgo

(The Virgin) August 21 to September 20

Ruled by: Mercury
Element: Earth
Character traits: Virgos are intelligent and have a great respect for higher education. They are not as emotional as other signs and may judge themselves and others too harshly. Virgos understand the art of conversation and do not complain about hard work. They can be pure of thought and perfectionists; but when their guard is down, they can have a childlike quality.

Libra ♎

(The Balance or Scales) September 21 to October 20

Ruled by: Venus
Element: Air
Character traits: Libras are delightful companions. They take great joy in beauty and delight in group efforts. It is important they keep their scales balanced emotionally. They shine in social situations; and when they find the right partner, they are unwavering in their affections.

Scorpio ♏

(The Scorpion) October 21 to November 20

Ruled by: Mars
Element: Water
Character traits: A powerful force drives Scorpios. They can have great passion for people or situations; but when it comes to romantic love, temptations can occur if he or she does not think logically. This sign is intense, magnetic, and fascinating.

Sagittarius ♐

(The Archer) November 21 to December 20

Ruled by: Jupiter
Element: Fire
Character traits: People born under the Sagittarius sign are philosophical and make exceptional marriage and business partners. They are adventurous and have a positive nature, offering quality advice to assist anyone. These kind souls are energetic and have a quick wit.

Capricorn

(The Goat) December 21 to January 20

Ruled by: Saturn

Element: Earth

Character traits: Capricorns are the hardest-working sign of the zodiac. They are very independent. They are achievers in the highest sense, demonstrating great depth and sincerity. They are physically alluring, but cautious when it comes to romantic issues. To be a Capricorn is to be successful, because they make it happen through pure ambition.

Aquarius

(The Water Bearer) January 21 to February 20

Ruled by: Uranus

Element: Air

Character traits: Aquarius people are gifted in many areas and often achieve fame. They do best when they listen to their own feelings and do not take the advice of others.

A sign of intuition, they are seers. They are not loud or demanding. They are modest and unselfish, yet sometimes can appear aloof.

Pisces

(The Fishes) February 21 to March 20

Ruled by: Jupiter and Neptune

Element: Water

Character traits: Pisces people are social butterflies. Emotional, sentimental, and romantic qualities make this sign popular. They tend to have a difficult time making decisions—to the point of feeling a bit sorry for themselves. A Pisces has the ability to shine light into dark corners and can be a supportive friend.

Element Meanings in Western Astrology

FIRE: (Aries, Leo, and Sagittarius) The fire signs are happy and energetic people.

EARTH: (Taurus, Virgo, and Capricorn) The earth signs are "down to earth," have common sense, and are practical.

AIR: (Gemini, Libra, and Aquarius) The air signs are those that contemplate ideas and situations deeply.

WATER: (Cancer, Scorpio, and Pisces) The water signs are emotional, perceptive, and sensitive.

Note to the reader: Please bear in mind that I have presented only the basics in the most general format in regard to Chinese astrology, Western astrology, and numerology. I recommend you seek further information if you want in-depth analysis of these subjects.

Conclusion

When we can learn to channel the energy of the Moon and become familiar with the power of the individual phases, we can start to transform this vitality into our own lives.

By using spells as a springboard to project your thoughts, you put your thoughts into action in an orderly manner. A spell creates an overall climate in your mind and is just a starting point to focus on what you want. For serious individuals who accept that there are things beyond the physical realm, the spells will be successful, as they have been for me and others who are like-minded. Henry Ford once said, "If you think you can or you think you can't, you're right!"

Bibliography

Abell, George O., and Barry Singer. *Science and the Paranormal.* New York: Charles Scribner's Sons, 1981.

Arnold, Larry, and Sandy Nevius. *The Reiki Handbook.* Harrisburg, PA: ParaScience International, 1982.

Biedermann, Hans. *Dictionary of Symbolism.* New York: Facts on File, Inc., 1989.

Cayce, Hugh Lynn. *Venture Inward.* New York: Paperback Library, 1964.

Dunwich, Gerina. *The Magick of Candle Burning.* Secaucus, NJ: Carol Publishing Group, 1989.

Greenhouse, Herbert B. *The Book of Psychic Knowledge.* New York: Taplinger Publishing Co., 1973.

Hewitt, William W. *Astrology for Beginners.* St. Paul, MN: Lewellyn Publications, 1993.

Hoffman, Enid. *Develop Your Psychic Skills.* Gloucester, MA: Para Research, 1981.

Hope, Murry. *Practical Techniques of Psychic Self-Defense.* New York: St. Martin's Press, 1983.

Howard, Jane M. *Commune with the Angels.* Virginia Beach, VA: A.R.E. Press, 1992.

Kennedy, David Daniel. *Feng Shui for Dummies.* Foster City, CA: IDG Books Worldwide, Inc., 2001.

Talesco, Patricia. *Love Magic.* Freedom, CA: The Crossing Press, 1999.

Silbey, Uma. *The Complete Crystal Guidebook.* San Francisco, CA: U-Read Publications, 1986.

Sullivan, Kevin. *The Crystal Handbook.* New York: Penguin Group, 1987.

Time Life Books. *Search for the Soul.* Alexandria, VA: 1989.

Index

D

E

F

G

H

I

J

K

L

M